C000178283

This is an authentic explorat
the Christian discipleship we
actually live out our day-to-c
all at once confronts, challenges and encourages twenty-
century believers to 'keep on keeping on' in their walk, no matter
how far short of the standard they fall. Having read *Undivided*,
I feel that the words 'Mind the gap' will never have the same
meaning again!
Jill Garrett, Director of Leadership and Employee Engagement at
LT Consulting

The wisdom of experience combines with biblical insight in this
accessible and practical book.
Julian Hardyman, Senior Pastor, Eden Baptist Church, Cambridge

Graham Hooper reminds us that we are called to follow the
Master, who was unafraid of facing the reality of life all around
him and was only too willing to connect with it fully. Jesus calls
us to live in the same way. This book offers a vision of holy living
and whole living.
Neil Hudson, Director of 'Imagine' at LICC and author of Imagine
Church

This is one of those key, life-changing books for which we have
been waiting for a long time. It is born out of a lifetime's practice
of living as a Christian in the cut and thrust of the professional
world and has all the hallmarks of proven wisdom and
experience. In itself the book bridges the gap between the whole
spectrum of biblical truth and faith, on the one hand, and the
challenges, frustrations and opportunities of its application to life
in the real world of the twenty-first century, on the other.
Pulsating with honesty, integrity, realism and faith, it is a masterly
match of clear biblical teaching with the issues of life today,
especially in the workplace. For anyone longing to live more
authentically for Christ in today's culture, this is essential reading.
Not only will it refresh, challenge and inspire, but its message
will transform our experience of everyday living as God's people,
in God's world, in our generation. I commend it most warmly.
David Jackman, former President, Proclamation Trust

GRAHAM HOOPER

UNDIVIDED

Closing the faith–life gap

INTER-VARSITY PRESS
Norton Street, Nottingham NG7 3HR, England
Email: ivp@ivpbooks.com
Website: www.ivpbooks.com

© Graham Hooper 2013

Graham Hooper has asserted his right under the Copyright, Design and
Patents Act 1988 to be identified as Author of this work.

All rights reserved. No part of this publication may be reproduced, stored in
a retrieval system, or transmitted, in any form or by any means, electronic,
mechanical, photocopying, recording or otherwise, without the prior
permission of the publisher or the Copyright Licensing Agency.

Unless otherwise stated, Scripture quotations are taken from the Holy
Bible, New International Version® Anglicized, NIV® Copyright © 1979,
1984, 2011 by Biblica, Inc.® Used by permission. All rights reserved
worldwide.

Scripture quotations marked NKJV are from the New King James Version.
Copyright © 1982 by Thomas Nelson, Inc. Used by permission.

The quotation on p. 8 is from Bob Dylan, 'Blind Willie McTell'. Copyright
©1983, Special Rider Music. Administered by Sony / ATV Music Publishing.
All rights reserved. Used by permission.

The extract from the song 'In Christ Alone' on pp. 24–25, by Stuart
Townend and Keith Getty. Copyright ©2001, Thankyou Music. Adm. by
worshiptogether.com songs excl. UK & Europe, adm. by Kingswaysongs,
a division of David C Cook tym@kingsway.co.uk. Used by permission.

First published 2013

British Library Cataloguing in Publication Data
A catalogue record for this book is available from the British Library.

ISBN: 978–1–84474–624–8

Set in Dante 12/15pt
Typeset in Great Britain by CRB Associates, Potterhanworth, Lincolnshire
Printed in Great Britain by Ashford Colour Press Ltd, Gosport, Hampshire

*Inter-Varsity Press publishes Christian books that are true to the Bible and that
communicate the gospel, develop discipleship and strengthen the church for its
mission in the world.*

*Inter-Varsity Press is closely linked with the Universities and Colleges Christian
Fellowship, a student movement connecting Christian Unions in universities and
colleges throughout Great Britain, and a member movement of the International
Fellowship of Evangelical Students. Website: www.uccf.org.uk*

Contents

Teach me your way, Lord,
that I may rely on your faithfulness;
give me an undivided heart,
that I may fear your name.
(Psalm 86:11)

Acknowledgments

I would like to thank the two commissioning editors at IVP: Kate Byrom who first believed in this project and got me started, and Sam Parkinson whose gracious, wise and sometimes challenging suggestions made this a much better book than it might otherwise have been.

I am grateful to others who have reviewed and advised along the way: John Folmar and Mark Greene, both of whom read early drafts of some chapters and made helpful suggestions, and particularly David Jackman who reviewed the whole draft manuscript and added his support and invaluable advice.

I would also like to thank all those in different countries and churches who have enriched my life and who are mentioned directly or indirectly in this book.

Most of all, I thank Clare, Joy and Mark for their unwavering love and support, and Sue, my wife, who knows all the gaps in my life better than anyone else on the planet, and goes on loving me.

Thank you.

Preface

Well, God is in His heaven
and we all want what's His
But power and greed and corruptible seed
Seem to be all that there is
Bob Dylan[1]

There is a gap between the way we would like life to be and the way it actually is; a gap between who we are and who we would like to be; a gap between the Christianity that is professed in churches and the Christianity that is practised by many churchgoers. There is a gap between us and God.

This book is about these gaps.

It is for anyone who is struggling to live out their Christian faith in day-to-day life; to integrate the sacred and the secular, the religious and the routine; to make sense of what we say and do 'at church' . . . and relate that to how we live our lives the rest of the time.

Graham Hooper
Dubai
August 2012

PART 1:
EXPOSING THE GAP

1. The problem

I never cease to be amazed and amused by the gap between the public face of what's known as Christianity and the way things actually are for people who call themselves Christians.
Adrian Plass[1]

Questions

It was after church one Sunday morning, about ten years ago. I had left feeling strangely unsettled and dissatisfied.

Was it the fault of the preacher: his voice, his style, the length of the sermon and its content? Was it the form of service? Perhaps it was the worship leader, who seemed particularly annoying that day, or the selection of music? Was it other people in the congregation that I found difficult to relate to? Or could it be me? Was it that I was simply in the wrong mood, spiritually out of tune, or just plain depressed?

Driving home, I found myself observing people going about their secular Sunday morning business: jogging, gardening, car washing, relaxing with a coffee and a newspaper. I felt overwhelmed by the huge gap between my one-hour experience in church and what was going on outside in the world. Clearly there was a 'dis-connect' somewhere. How was it that the great majority of people seemed to be so uninterested in the Christian gospel?

Certainly most people had other priorities that Sunday morning. Why? Surely not because they were particularly lazy or sinful. Was it that their material world was so comfortable that they felt no need of God, at least until they faced a personal crisis? Statistically, it was likely that a large number professed to believe in God or to possess some sort of faith. So was it just that they didn't see the relevance of the church and Christianity to their lives?

Was that because of the poor quality and inconsistency of the witness of Christians they knew? Had they ever been confronted with the good news that there was a God who had made them and who loved them? Was the gap between what Christians professed to believe and how they actually behaved most of the time so big that the message of the gospel was being undermined? Sinful human nature is alive and well, even in the best of people. Was that why the majority of the population was outside the churches rather than inside that Sunday?

Back at work the next day, it was almost a relief to stop contemplating the meaning of life and get back to the routine. I quickly immersed myself again in the pressures of my job. Spiritual things were moved firmly onto the back burner. How was I to relate my church experience of the previous day to the pressures and challenges of my work as a manager in an engineering business? Perhaps the simplest thing was not to worry about it, just to keep church life and business separate. There seemed to me a big gap between church and work, between the Christianity professed in churches and the Christianity practised by many churchgoers, and I was not at all sure that I was closing that gap.

At home that evening, I watched the news on TV, with its usual catalogue of disaster, exploitation, violence and corruption. I felt helpless in the face of the gap between the world as it is and the world as it could be. Why didn't God 'wave a magic wand' and fix all the problems? What impact was the church making on the world's problems? What impact was I making? How much difference did my faith really make to the way I lived?

Why couldn't we achieve peace in the Middle East? Why couldn't people get on with one another? Closer to home, why was it that relationship problems sometimes made the work environment, and even family life, so complicated and difficult?

It is always easy to criticize others. But if I accepted Jesus' premise that the problem could be the log in my own eye rather than the speck in someone else's, then I also had to face up to the gap between the inconsistencies and shortcomings in my life and the person I wanted to be, at least in my better moments. Why did I find it so difficult to live consistently and to live up to God's standards? Like most people, I was reluctant to let my guard down and allow people to see the 'real me'. So I also had to face the gap between the way I wanted others to see me and who I really was.

At the root of all these problems lay the big question, the elephant in the room: Why did God often seem so far away? Why did he not seem to answer my prayers? Why was there such a gap between him and me?

How did he intend all these gaps to be closed?

Answers?

As I turned more and more to the Scriptures for answers, I found that, while I came to God with a long list of questions, he clearly had some to ask me! In the Bible we find that in many crunch situations God's Word to his people comes in the form of a question, one to which he clearly knows the answer. He asked Adam, 'Where are you?' (Genesis 3:9). He asked Cain, 'Where is your brother . . . ' (Genesis 4:9). He asked Elijah, 'What are you doing here . . . ?' (1 Kings 19:13). Jesus asked Peter, 'Do you love me . . . ?' (John 21:16). God wants us to face life's big questions.

It's easy to drive through life for long periods on cruise control. We can try to focus only on the positives and dodge the big issues, but at some point, maybe in a family or personal crisis, God will speak to us through his Word and by his Spirit, by asking us questions: 'Where are you really at?'; 'What is the state of your relationship with others?'; 'Do you really love and trust me . . . or is that just religious talk?'

God cares for us. So he calls us back from the religious fantasy world in which we sometimes like to operate to show us the reality of our lives as he sees them. We may try to paper over the gaps and pretend they are not there, but we are only kidding ourselves. The nagging feeling that all is not as it should be will not go away. Real crises in our lives quickly tear away the veneer of a merely superficial Christian faith and expose the gaps.

Studying the Scriptures, I found it very encouraging that God's people down the centuries have all struggled with these gaps. Many of the Old Testament psalms are songs of praise, but there are also many songs of questioning, of desperation, even of anguish. They are written by believers who sensed a big gap between themselves and their God (Psalm 88); people who could not understand why the life of faith was such a struggle when others seemed to have it so easy (Psalm 73); people who questioned why God seemed to ignore their cry for help (Psalm 13); people having to face up to their own spectacular failures (Psalm 51). In other words, they were written by people like us who were asking big questions and not always getting the answers they wanted. At least they were being honest with themselves, and with God. Let's look and learn.

As you read this, I hope it challenges you to face the gaps that are so obviously there, rather than go on living in some unreal world in which you never ask any of your biggest questions. We need to *ask* the big questions, even if we don't receive all the answers. We also need to *face* the big questions with which God confronts us. We need to live authentic lives.

Learning on the job

My job has taken me to live and work in several different countries. My wife and I have had the privilege of belonging to churches of various denominations and in different cultures. What follows in this book has come from spending most of my adult life as a Christian working in the secular world. I try to relate the Bible to life, to link the secular with the sacred, to make sense of what we do and say in church, and how we live the rest of the time.

It is a work in progress. It does not produce, or even promise, a quick-fix solution, because there isn't one this side of eternity. But as I share what I have learned, and go on learning from God, through the Scriptures, through other Christians (and non-Christians), and in life's school of hard knocks, I hope you will be able to relate to these gaps and be encouraged, as you experience God working in your life, and in the world, to close them.

When I came to faith in Christ in my twenties, I was told that to grow as a new Christian I needed to read the Bible, to pray and to join a church. True! But that is not the whole story. What I was *not* told so clearly, and what I have since learned, is that we grow closer to God as we go through tough times in which our faith and hope are tested. Looking back on his life, the apostle Paul wrote these magnificent words: 'I have learned the secret of being content in any and every situation'

(Philippians 4:12). How did he learn that? Not in a book or a lifestyle seminar. No. He learned it through personal experience of hardship and testing, in which he had to rely wholly on God. Even Jesus, the perfect Son of God, 'learned obedience from what he suffered' (Hebrews 5:8). We have much to learn.

But it is not only through tough times that we learn and grow. God calls us to make a difference in the world. As we take on tasks and responsibilities to which we believe God is calling us, whether at work, in the community or in the church, we find enjoyment and fulfilment. We also learn to rely increasingly on God's guidance and daily strength. As our faith is stretched in that way, we learn about, and experience, the power of God, and so the gap between us closes. We grow closer to him.

Gaps and compartments

It is all too easy (not to mention a massive cop-out) to compartmentalize our lives. We often speak about our 'Christian life', our 'prayer life', our 'church life', our 'married life', our 'secular life', our 'family life', even our 'sex life', in a way which unintentionally separates that which is really a whole. The result of the gaps between these compartments is that we increasingly divorce the religious part of our lives from the rest. We start to become one person at church and another at work or at home. Inevitably, then, our lives make little difference for good.

It might be convenient if life could be divided up like that into multiple different compartments, each with its own rules of behaviour. However, real life is not like that. Problems do not confront us one at a time in an orderly pattern, like a succession of waves approaching the shoreline. We don't typically face relationship problems on Thursday, work problems on Friday, personal issues on Saturday, religious matters on Sunday, and so on. No. Sometimes life is like a stormy maelstrom, with waves crashing in on us from all directions at once.

Indeed, you may be confronted by a whole range of spiritual, personal, relationship and work issues right now. Any twenty-four-hour period of life may include a wide range of feelings and experiences – some good times: laughter, satisfaction in a task well done, reconciliation, times of prayer, and a new sense of the grace of God. But in that same day you may have to cope with many personal battles: worry, difficult relationships, pain, frustration and stress. If you are a Christian, then you probably have a few church-related issues thrown in for good measure.

When you analyse the problems in your life, you probably find that many of them are interrelated. Perhaps your bad day at work was caused by an argument at home. And maybe that relationship problem, in turn, was partially caused by your own doubts, anxieties, feelings of guilt, and a growing distance between you and God. Perhaps the emptiness of your spiritual life is bound up tightly with the conflicts you are experiencing and a sense of missing out on life's best. We can quickly feel disconnected from God and from one another, and divided inside. These are the gaps! Our church experience and spiritual life can easily become an unreal sideshow or an escape from the 'real business' of life. Our time at work can become totally divorced from our experience at church. If you are a professing Christian, or claim any religious conviction, you may still be going through the motions of worship and prayer, but with a feeling that your faith is increasingly unrelated to the rest of your life.

How are we to deal with all these interrelated problems? It seems impossible to tackle them all at once, but piecemeal solutions are inadequate. We need to bring the whole of our lives, with all their compartments, to God.

The integrity of Jesus

Let's take a moment to contrast our inconsistent, compart-mentalized and disintegrated lives with the wholeness and consistency of Jesus. In thirty-three years on this earth, he showed himself to be, uniquely, a whole person. What came out was what was inside. His words and actions were entirely consistent with his character. His honesty, his compassion, his hatred of injustice and hypocrisy were simply expressions of his true self. He was a man of total integrity.

This amazing quality stands in stark contrast to the values of the world of business and politics, in which perception counts more than truth. Spin doctoring, imaging, market pos-itioning, key messaging, how to mislead without actually lying, how to portray things in the most favourable light possible while massively under-emphasizing the other side of the picture: this is the reality of political and business life in the twenty-first century. At its core, this is simply creating a gap between reality and communication. At its worst, it is dishonesty.

Honesty

One of the great characteristics of Jesus that does not receive a lot of airtime from writers and preachers is his *honesty*. He spoke directly and with great insight, using words that went straight to the hearts of his hearers. That is why his enemies, the religious leaders who lost out when the status quo was disturbed, hated him. They were jealous of him because he was everything they were not. They saw him as a serious threat to their power, and so they hounded him to death.

In his famous Sermon on the Mount (Matthew 5 – 7), Jesus calls for *honesty in worship*. If you are angry with someone, or if you have given someone reason to hold a grudge against you, he says, don't bother coming to worship God. First put the relationship right, and *then* come to worship (see Matthew 5:22–24). I sometimes wonder, if every church was challenged with this at the beginning of each service, would half the congregation need to leave, to work on repairing relationships? We do need to take this seriously. Are there some personal visits or phone calls we need to make to put things right with people before we next go to church?

True worship of God is inextricably linked to our God-given daily life. He does not mean us to divorce the experience of the one-hour worship service in church from the other 167 hours in the week spent in the home, the school, the workplace or the shopping centre. According to the apostle Paul, it is committing our *whole* life in service that is the real act of worship (Romans 12:1–2).

Jesus also calls for *honesty in our estimation of our own character*. He points out the gap between mere *outward* observance of laws and *inward* obedience. In God's eyes, he says, these should be one and the same thing. If you want to kill someone, then the sin in your life is the same as if you had actually killed. Of course, the effects on others, and the consequences for you and others between the thought and the act, may be totally different. But in God's eyes there is sin in the evil desire, as well as in the act. He will not allow us the luxury of thinking ourselves good and holy just because we have not *done* certain things, when we are at least guilty of *thinking* them (Matthew 5:21–30).

Consistency

Jesus also demands *consistency* as well as honesty: consistency, that is – not boring predictability. He calls for the consistent application of our faith to life. When I think of this quality, I remember my friend Rob, who was a great example to me in this way. He was described by one of his colleagues as 'a man who takes Christ to work with him', a wonderful accolade for a very shy individual. But he was someone with great personal warmth, quiet strength and a lovely sense of humour, whose faith clearly influenced the way he worked. How?

He was an electrician, responsible for maintenance of a defence installation. His consistently high standards of workmanship and his strict ethical values won him the respect of his peers. If you were looking for someone you could rely on to get a job done, or a friend to share a confidence with, someone to be there when it mattered, then Rob was that man. He was also always courteous and respectful to those he met, whatever their position in the hierarchy. In short, he was totally and consistently reliable, qualities that are like gold in any workplace and which reflect the character of God.

In his teaching, Jesus pointed out that in nature there is a *consistency between the type of tree and the fruit it bears*. He asks, rhetorically, 'Do people pick grapes from thorn-bushes, or figs from thistles?' (Matthew 7:16). Apple trees always and only produce apples, not pears or oranges.

Jesus looked in vain for the same consistency in those who claimed to be God's people, but whose lives produced fruit that showed otherwise. Jesus also exposed the *inconsistency* of those who expect God to forgive them but will not forgive others, people who are hypercritical and judgmental of the failings of others, but who choose to ignore their own, far greater faults (Matthew 18:23–35). In the prayer Jesus taught us (Matthew 6:9–13), we are reminded to forgive others *as we ourselves are forgiven*. And in the so-called 'golden rule' for interpersonal relationships, we are to treat others *as we would have them treat us* (Matthew 7:12).

James, in his letter to the early church, is puzzled by a similar inconsistency (see James 3:9–12). He observes that in nature the same spring does not produce fresh water one moment and salty the next. How is it, then, that human beings can speak words of encouragement one moment and curse and swear the next? How is it that one moment we can mouth words of praise and worship of God and the next say things that reveal a much darker side of our character? What is inside us eventually comes out, however much we try to suppress or hide it. If we are rotten inside, our lives will eventually produce rotten fruit: lies, deceit, betrayal, selfishness in our behaviour at work and at home. It is what comes *out* of us that defiles us, said Jesus, not what goes in (Mark 7:15).

Inside each of us there is something rotten – the Bible calls it sin. It is destructive of personality and relationships.

Wholeness

Wholeness means a relationship with God which expresses itself in honest relationships with other people and in living a godly life in this ungodly world. Jesus emphasized that this quality is not just a matter of regulatory compliance with the 'do nots': not killing, not stealing, not committing adultery, and so on. It is about having inner purity of thought and motive (see Matthew 5:21–22, 27–28, 33–34, 38–39). It is about the application of faith to the whole of life, seven days a week.

Jesus clearly hated the gaps between what we say we believe and how we actually live and relate to one another. He asked his disciples in some amazement, 'Why do you call me, "Lord, Lord," and do not do what I say?' (Luke 6:46) – another of Jesus' big questions! He confronted them with the gap between their professed belief and the way they lived.

How do we compare?

In practice, we often find that living at the level of honesty, consistency and integrity shown by Jesus, and called for by Jesus, is too hard. So we give up and sink down to a mediocre level of Christian experience. We simply become accustomed to the gaps as being 'the way things are'. Stephen Rand made this observation from his experience of working in many poor communities around the world, and from struggling to inspire 'comfortable Christians' to get more involved in the needs of others: 'I sat on the balcony looking down literally and metaphorically on those who seemed to have found a faith that allowed such comfortable complacency. I nearly got lost in *the gap* between the church and the real world.'[2] If we allow ourselves to drift down to a state of acceptance of this particular gap, we should not be surprised that our lives have so little impact for good on others, that our Christian profession has so little credibility, or that people mock the glaring inconsistencies in our lives.

The gap between us and God

'I always knew that there was a gap between me and God.' Those were the words used by a young woman in our church in Dubai to describe her life before coming to faith in Christ. They express, very succinctly, the fact presented in the Bible – that at the root of the 'gap problems' we have thought about so far is the gap that exists between us and God.

Actually, there are two massive gaps. First, there is a quite obvious gap between us and God, in that we cannot see him. Human beings can communicate with one another via Twitter, Facebook, email, text messaging, letter or telephone, but the best communication is still face to face, so that we can observe the other person's body language and sense the way in which they respond to each situation and to what we say, and we can see the expression in their eyes as they speak to us. People may meet and even fall in love via the internet, but human beings still communicate best face to face. So if we cannot see God, we have a seemingly unbridgeable gap, a permanent limit on the quality of any possible relationship. This gap, 'the visibility gap', is obvious to us.

However, according to the Bible, there is an even more formidable gap to be bridged, one that is less obvious, and which many non-Christians deny is real or relevant to the world's problems. There is a gap between the holy character of God and the weakness, pride and selfishness of the people he has made. The prophet Isaiah articulated this problem very clearly: 'But your iniquities have separated you from your God' (Isaiah 59:2).

When I was searching for the truth in my early twenties, I thought only in self-centred terms. I thought it was all about me. *I* wanted peace of mind. *I* wanted the satisfaction of knowing what life was all about. It was only later that I began to learn that this very self-centredness was separating me from God. I began to see that I had to centre my life on God, not the other way round.

The apostle Paul describes the effects of separation from God by reminding his fellow Christians to reflect on what they used to be: 'Remember that at that time you were separate from Christ, excluded from citizenship in Israel and foreigners to the covenants of the promise, without hope and without God in the world' (Ephesians 2:12). This is the desperate plight of humankind: hopeless, godless and without answers that make sense of death – separated from God by a huge gap.

Alienation from God is the root cause of all the 'gap problems' we face. By nature, we don't know God or fully understand him. We try to reach up to him, but our natural sinfulness and human limitations get in the way. As we struggle to build relationships and become better people, we repeatedly fail to hit our target. Life is not as it should be. Life is certainly not as we would like it to be. We do not have the answers, and God seems far away, if he is there at all.

So what's the good news . . . ?

At the centre of the gospel message is the fact that Jesus, in his life, death and resurrection, dealt decisively with the two main gap problems we face.

In his life, he showed us what God is like (John 1:18; 14:9), enabling us to know him, even though we cannot see him.

In his death, he carried the oppressive load of our sin in his own body on the cross. He paid the price for our sins that separate us from God. In that act, he bridged the gap between us and God.

In his resurrection and ascension, he showed that the will of God, and the power of God, will prevail over sin, evil and even death. Good news!

There in the ground His body lay,
Light of the world by darkness slain;
Then bursting forth in glorious day,
Up from the grave He arose again!
And as he stands in victory,

Sin's curse has lost its grip on me;
For I am His and He is mine –
Bought with the precious blood of Christ.[3]

When we are honest with God and with ourselves, when we respond in faith to the love of God shown in Jesus Christ, we are forgiven and reconciled to him. This is the first crucial step in closing the gap between us and God, but it is only the first step. As Christian believers, we still face these two fundamental gaps. We cannot yet see God, so we are called to live by faith (Hebrews 11:1). Also, we remain sinful, self-centred people. Christian though we may be, forgiven, justified, reconciled and redeemed, our lives are still miles away from the integrity, honesty, compassion and selflessness of Christ.

Thank God, at this point he has more good news to bring us. We can experience his power and presence *in the daily routine of life*. The Bible tells us how our lives can be progressively changed by the Holy Spirit of God, as we begin to live in faith and hope. It tells us how the gaps between people are closed in loving, committed relationships at home, at work and in the church; how the world is changed through changed people, whose work is part of their worship, and who make a difference for good to the lives of those they encounter. The Bible shows us how to deal with success and failure. It encourages us to press on to obey God's call on our life and not to give up. It also points us forward to the day when all gaps will be closed, every question answered, and we shall see him and be like him forever.

The rest of this book is devoted to bringing the gospel to bear on these gaps.

God, in Jesus Christ, has acted to bridge the gap between us. That God will one day close that gap forever is my ultimate source of joy and purpose. That God acts in my life now, and in the world and in the church, with all its flaws, is, to use the cliché, what gets me out of bed in the mornings.

Reflection

Where in your life is the greatest gap between what you profess to believe about God and how you live?

How can that gap be closed?

How can you live a more consistently 'integrated' life?

PART 2:
THE GAP IS CLOSED . . .
WHEN WE ARE CHANGED

2. Facing the truth

You have searched me, LORD,
and you know me.
(Psalm 139:1)

The gap between what we are really like and how others perceive us

How do you react when you hear a recording of your voice or see yourself on film? For most of us, it's a nasty shock to realize how others must perceive us. Surely I don't sound like that! Surely I don't look as fat/old/ugly as that!

How you appear to others and how you see yourself are different. Think of the judgments you often pass on others, almost unthinkingly: 'Look at that guy's pot belly . . . why doesn't he start exercising?'; 'Is that girl anorexic? She's so thin!'

Now imagine for a moment that others are passing similar judgment on you, not only on your physical appearance, but on your character. Imagine if people could see *you* as you really are – all the unworthy thoughts and petty jealousies, the scheming to pay back people who have hurt you, the self-pity, the arrogance – not a pretty sight. Perhaps what would be most surprising, if 'all was revealed' in that way, would be to see the doubts and insecurities of people who seem success-ful, confident and poised on the outside, those who appear to others as strong and self-reliant, but who inwardly suffer from self-doubt.

Many organizations put their employees through an annual performance assessment, usually prior to a salary review. Some businesses include a 360-degree performance appraisal (like the Johari window process[1]) in which employees are reviewed by their peers, as well as by those above and below them in the hierarchy. This can be a chastening and humbling experience, as people discover the gap between how they see themselves and how others see them. We may have one view of our character, and how well we are doing on the scorecard of life, but those above us, beneath us and alongside us may see us very differently.

For all of us there is a gap. Why? Because we are blind to many of our own faults and weaknesses, though they may be obvious to those with whom we live and work. But it's also because many of us create and carefully preserve layers of protection, so that people cannot see us as we really are. We fear that, if others could see us like that, then they would no longer like us, respect us or look up to us, so we are reluctant to let down the barriers.

David Cornwall, aka John le Carré, was interviewed in a BBC documentary, *The Secret Path*, first broadcast in 2000. The great author, and former intelligence agent, looked back on his dysfunctional family life and his education as a boarder at a top school in England. He recalled how he was living two lives, one at school and one at home: 'The actual gulf between Sherbourne, with its very high church orthodoxy as it then was, and the chaos of domestic life, and the terribly funny rackety scenes we lived, that gulf became almost unbridgeable and absurd . . . ' For many people like David Cornwall, the tension involved in living two lives is intolerable. But when one of these lives has a religious dimension, it is perhaps even worse. If I try to keep my 'Christian life' entirely separate from my 'social life', I am like an actor trying to play two different roles on two different stages at the same time. When the gap between these roles gets wide enough, and the tension strong enough, then something snaps and life gets messy. Pretending to be other than we are is not a sustainable lifestyle. I first learned this lesson as a young Christian, when I was asked to stand up in church and speak to a congregation which included three of my workmates. My two 'roles' quickly had to merge into one!

God's searching diagnosis

But what really matters is not how others see us, nor how we see ourselves, but how God sees us. He made us and he knows us better than we know ourselves. God wants us to see things as he sees them. This surely underpins our whole understanding of God's revelation of himself. He wants us to understand that the core of the world's problems is not primarily political, economic or social; it is spiritual and moral, due to human sinfulness, resulting in a gap between us and God.

At the personal level, he wants us to understand the state of our lives and the status of our relationship with him *as he sees it*, not as we might deceive ourselves into imagining it. We need to hear God's diagnosis of our problems. It is all too easy for us to have an unrealistic view of the quality of our lives, our relationships, our worship and our witness, one that does not correlate with how others see us and which is miles apart from how God sees us.

One of my daughters, at the age of seventeen, started to experience weight loss and raging thirst. It was clear that she was sick, but with what? The doctor carried out various tests and found her blood sugar was at dangerously high levels. She had type 1 diabetes. The doctor confronted her with the brutal truth that her pancreas was no longer producing any insulin and that for the rest of her life she would need to inject herself with insulin in order to survive. She quickly had to learn to monitor the sugar levels in her body through several blood tests each day, and to control those levels with four daily insulin injections and a strictly controlled diet.

On the day of her diagnosis, she was jolted right out of her comfort zone and confronted with the truth that she had a life-threatening disease. If she did not comply with the doctor's instructions, she would die. There was little opportunity to go into denial.

Looking back, she could have responded to her health problem in one of four ways. She could have just tried to ignore the symptoms and hoped to recover naturally. She could have relied on well-meaning advice from friends to rest and change her diet. She could have tried to prescribe her own treatment, drinking more and more water to quench her thirst. But if she had gone down any of these routes, she would not have survived. Diabetes is a serious disease. Thank God, she chose the fourth option. She went to a doctor, who recognized the symptoms, diagnosed the problem and prescribed the treatment.

How do we react when we start to become aware of problems in life generally: when we are not finding satisfaction in our work, when we are at odds with those we live with, when we are not at peace with ourselves, and when God seems far away? Typically, we respond in one or other of these same four ways.

We can go into denial and convince ourselves that the issue is not something we need to deal with, or we might pretend that the problem does not exist at all. The New Testament presents several examples of people who were unwilling to face the truth with which they were confronted, individuals who were brought face to face with reality but who then backed away, unwilling to change, unwilling to accept God's claim on their lives. There was the 'rich young ruler' who loved his wealth too much to follow Jesus (Matthew 19:16–24). There was Felix the governor who had listened to the apostle Paul talk about 'righteousness, self-control and the judgment to come', at which point Felix became fearful and cut Paul off: 'That's enough for now! You may leave. When I find it convenient, I will send for you' (Acts 24:25). Paul had touched a nerve. Felix sensed the power of God starting to intrude into his life, and his response was to push it away, to go into denial. Both of these men had recognized the gaps in their lives and at first had seemed interested in understanding how God could close them. But when the crunch came, they did not want to face up to the truth.

We might prefer to look inwards, to rely on our own intelligence, abilities and spiritual resources to solve our problems. That's the road most advocated and most travelled in Western popular culture.

Our third option is to turn to others for help. Twitter and Facebook have added a whole new dimension to this option. If I were to stop writing now and use one of the social networks to ask advice on a relationship problem, I could be bombarded with comments from around the world within minutes. Certainly a mark of wisdom is being humble enough to accept advice and correction from others (e.g. Proverbs 19:20). But we also need wisdom and discernment to sift the advice we receive. In any event, such advice is unlikely to be infallible – even from a close friend.

When we face the big questions, the life-and-death problems, relying on our own resources or on the advice of others will not be enough; nor will hoping our problems will simply disappear. The most important choice we can make when confronted by any of the gaps we have talked about thus far is *to turn to God*. He alone can give us a comprehensive diagnosis of our problems and administer the treatment.

How do we do that? We ask him in prayer, as the psalmist did, to show us the true state of our lives:

> Search me, God, and know my heart;
>   test me and know my anxious thoughts.
> See if there is any offensive way in me,
>   and lead me in the way everlasting.
> (Psalm 139:23–24)

At the same time, we are to open God's Word and ask him to speak to us by his Spirit. As we do so, we will find that the Bible itself is a diagnostic tool. It is described as a *light* which shines into the dark places and shows us how to live (Psalm 119:105); it is likened to a *mirror* which reflects back to us what we really look like (James 1:23–25), and a *sharp sword* that pierces right to the heart, cutting through the layers of hypocrisy and self-deception with which we cover ourselves (Hebrews 4:12). The Bible reminds us that, 'Nothing in all creation is hidden from God's sight. Everything is uncovered and laid bare before the eyes of him to whom we must give account' (Hebrews 4:13).

Truth revealed

The Bible, of course, is much more than God's diagnostic tool. It is a revelation of God himself: a revelation of his character, his plan, his power, justice, love and grace. The Bible shows us what God has done, what he is doing in the world and what he will yet do to close the gaps.

It was as a young man living in a tent in the East African bush that I first started to read the Bible seriously and realize its power as the Word of God. I had packed in my gear an unopened hardback New Testament, received as a prize at school, which I thought would be useful for pressing flat my family photos.

Rocked by a long letter from a hippy friend who had come to faith in Christ, I opened the New Testament and started to read. Perversely, I started at the end, in the book of Revelation. I still remember the powerful impact of the words: ' "I am the Alpha and the Omega," says the Lord God, "who is, and who was, and who is to come, the Almighty" ' (Revelation 1:8). It was a life-changing moment. God had begun it all. God would end it all. God was real. He was alive. He was the ultimate frame of reference for life. I was brought face to face with the truth.

Over the years since, I have been thankful for the countless times when the Bible has been to me like a light to guide my way, a mirror showing me what I am really like and a sword that cuts right to the depth of my soul.

Accountability

It is not just that we are subject to God's performance review in order to 'lift our game', or to God's diagnosis, in which he prescribes treatments for our problems. There is a deeper truth. We are ultimately accountable to God for how we spend our lives. One day we will have to stand before him to give an account of our lives. We won't be able to hide then; so it's pointless trying to hide now.

We like to call God to account, but on that day he will be the one asking the questions. How well have we measured up to his holy standard? How have we used the gifts and opportunities he has given us? How faithful have we been to what was entrusted to us? How well have we cared for our fellow creatures?

Why do many find the idea that we will all have to face God's judgment so hard to accept? Accountability and assessment are part of life, whether exams for the student, or tax returns for the individual and business. Corporations have a duty of care under law and are accountable to their customers and to the community. Public servants are accountable for protecting the public interest. In a democracy, even politicians are accountable, to the electorate. Company boards are accountable to their shareholders and to the regulatory authorities. All of us are accountable to the authorities to pay taxes and keep the law. And we are all accountable to God.

In the light of this, we need to face up *now* to the reality of the gaps in our lives. They show how far we are from being the people God has called us to be. Recognizing the gaps is one thing. If we are to be changed, we also need to face the truth about ourselves as we really are. We need to submit ourselves to God's performance review, to his diagnosis and treatment, and to acknowledge our accountability to him. As we do so, we will also begin to understand more of the grace of God offered to us through Jesus Christ. We will begin to experience for ourselves his forgiveness and renewing power. Then, as we commit ourselves to living differently, with the spiritual strength and power that God alone provides, we will be changed.

Facing up to, and accepting, God's truth is not a one-off event, or even a weekly event. It's an ongoing process of change. I have learned that God deals with me by a variety of means: in reading Scripture, through the pressures of daily life and through the rebuke or challenge of someone close to me. If we have a spouse, a family member or a close friend who will be honest with us, we are blessed. If we have people around us who will keep pointing us back to God, we are doubly blessed.

During my time here in Dubai, every Saturday morning I have met with a group of Christian men from many different countries, to read the Scriptures and pray. As we share together our challenges in relating the Bible to our lives at work, to our relationships at home and to more personal issues, so our friendship has been strengthened. In a very positive way, we challenge one another to be honest before God and, in doing so, we find encouragement and strength to live out a more authentic Christian life at work and at home. One morning one of the guys, who had been absent from the group for several weeks, confessed that his driving ambition to establish his retail business had squeezed out any time for prayer and worship. Spiritually he was 'running on empty'. He broke down in tears and left the room for a few minutes to compose himself. On his return, he said, 'This group is a place of integrity.' That was one of the most honest, direct and moving statements I have ever heard said about any group, anywhere, Christian or otherwise. Do you belong to a group like that? Perhaps you need to join one . . . or start one.

Reflection

In what ways are you pretending to be something you are not?

Read Psalms 51 and 139. What do you need to put right with God?

3. Loving change

I am not what I ought to be, I am not what I want to be,
I am not what I hope to be in another world,
but still I am not what I once used to be and
by the Grace of God I am what I am.
John Newton[1]

The gap between how I want to live and how I actually live

It is the tensions within us that are the root of our difficulties in changing our lives for the better. We might be attracted by the beauty of the light, but, at the same time, we can't stop ourselves being fascinated by the darkness. Even the apostle Paul experienced this tension in his life. In his letter to the Romans, he describes the gap between the person he wants to be and the person he actually is: 'I do not understand what I do. For what I want to do I do not do, but what I hate I do' (Romans 7:15).

If you have ever made a resolution to change your behaviour for the better, you will know exactly what Paul means. Picture the following scene. You wake up in the morning, ashamed at the way you treated that work colleague you find difficult to get along with. You know that you should not have allowed that mild difference of opinion to degenerate into a full-on argument. Or at home, you know you could have been more thoughtful and encouraging to your wife when she was feeling tired at the end of her busy day. So in both cases, you resolve not to get irritable and angry, not to let the other person 'rub you up the wrong way' again. What happens? In the wear and tear of the busy day, you react to a word or action that does indeed rub you up the wrong way and out comes your usual response. What you do, to use Paul's words, is what you hate.

Or you decide you really must do something about that relationship that is going bad through leaving too many issues unresolved. You *want* to do the loving thing, the caring thing, but it's just too much effort and, after all, why should *you* be the one to make the first move? So you sit back and turn on the TV instead.

We *want* to be whole. We *want* the gap to be filled. We want to change . . . but how?

A divided heart

A prayer in the book of Psalms gets to the heart of this problem: 'Give me an undivided heart' (Psalm 86:11). This poet/songwriter knew that deep within himself he had a divided heart, a gap between the person he wanted to be and who he really was. He felt himself being pulled in different directions and he wanted more constancy in his life. He longed to be a whole person.

In the late 1960s, R. D. Laing's best-seller, *The Divided Self,*[2] was compulsory reading among my student friends. It made us question what was 'normal' and what was 'abnormal' in terms of human behaviour, and who was qualified to decide. It also made us think about how we are pressured into behaving in different ways in different circumstances in order to meet the expectations of others. The psalmist was not thinking of a psychiatric disorder when he called on God to unite his divided heart, but he realized that he was experiencing conflict *within* himself: he was being pulled in different directions by his own desires, by other people's expectations, by pressures from society and by God's call on his life.

Pamela Stephenson, the psychologist and the wife of entertainer Billy Connolly, made this observation about the tensions within people in public life whose lives are subject to greater scrutiny than most:

> Every person who comes to public attention experiences an alienation of self, the formation of a deeply unsettling chasm between his true inner self and his public persona. The danger lies not in the confusion of the two, as is commonly thought, but in the *widening gulf* between them.[3]

Even those of us who don't have to live in the spotlight can understand and experience the pressure to speak and act in ways which we know deep-down are contrary to our core beliefs: in other words, we try to be someone other than ourselves.

The writer of this psalm wanted to be whole, to know a unity, an integration of his whole being, a purity of heart – a life with no gaps. Every Christian has within them a God-given longing for a pure heart. That longing is itself a foretaste of the knowledge that the gap *will* be closed, that, by the grace of God, we will one day be like Christ.

I must confess to being a lover of Welsh music. The hymn 'Calon Lân' ('A Pure Heart') is still sung at Welsh international rugby matches in Cardiff. It's an interesting choice for a rugby match, in which a lot of very impure stuff is the norm! One verse from the English translation, which no doubt loses much of the poetry of the Welsh original, goes something like this:

> Evening and morning, my wish,
> Rising to heaven on the wings of a song
> For God, for the sake of my Saviour,
> To give me a pure heart.[4]

As I said, strange words to sing before a rugby game! But the sentiments express (albeit in flowery language) the God-given desire to be a better person, to have a pure heart, a whole heart.

Change is coming

Change is a fact of life. We can try to fight against it, but change will inevitably come. Organizations that want to change typically employ 'change agents', or 'change managers': people with the skills and drive (and sometimes other less attractive qualities) who are able to effect that change. We may resist change, particularly when it is imposed by others, and we feel threatened and insecure as familiar ways of living and working are taken away.

But change also provides new opportunities to test our faith, to stretch our abilities and to learn to rely on God. In business, people who progress in their careers are usually those who have learned to 'love change', rather than avoid it. In life generally, those who embrace change as an opportunity, rather than resist it as an enemy, tend to grow in character as they rise to meet new challenges.

God is the ultimate change manager. He wants us to change – for the better. That is often a painful process. Change is fundamental to being a Christian. We *have been* changed by the grace of God, in bringing us to repentance and faith in

Christ: 'If anyone is in Christ, the new creation has come: the old has gone, the new is here!' (2 Corinthians 5:17). We *are being* changed by the work of the Holy Spirit in our lives (2 Corinthians 3:18). We *will be* changed into his likeness at the end (1 Corinthians 15:51) when we see him.

If you want life to carry on in the same old way, as your wagon rolls down the same old ruts, then you have a problem: God wants to change you to be more like Christ. He wants to unite your divided heart. God's changes in our lives are changes for good. However, as we shall see in this chapter, it may be through difficult circumstances that he brings them about. Let's learn to 'love change', because it is change for good in our character that brings us closer to God, and because it is often the God-ordained changes in our circumstances which provide God-given opportunities for growth.

Reflecting the character of God into the world

What is God like? According to the Bible, he is a God of love, truth, justice and grace. He is a Creator, Redeemer, Reconciler and Restorer. He is not impressed by pomp, rank, wealth or education. He resists the proud and gives grace to the humble. He values honesty, faithfulness and justice very highly. He hates hypocrisy and loves generosity of spirit. Whenever we ourselves live out these values, or wherever we see these facets of God's character in others in this cynical and hard-bitten world, we experience the gap between us and God being closed.

Let me illustrate. During our years in Mauritius, we came to know a missionary called Wilf Green. He and his wife Marie had spent their lives serving in Malawi and South Africa. At an age when he could have retired, Wilf accepted a new position as minister of a church in a small working-class village in Mauritius. He was the most Christ-like man I have ever met.

During our time in Mauritius, we had a visitor from one of the villages in Malawi who remembered Wilf Green as a young man. He described the effect that Wilf had had on his community in these words: 'When I start work in the fields before dawn, it is cold and dark. Then the sun comes up and brings light and warms my back . . . that is what it was like when Wilf Green was here.'

What a beautiful picture of one individual reflecting the character of God into the world so that other people are blessed. To use New Testament language, that is a life which makes 'the teaching about God our Saviour attractive' (Titus 2:10).

For every hypocrite and for every person who makes it hard to believe in God, there is someone like Wilf Green, who shows by their life the character of God.

How can we become like that? The Bible's answer is that, on the one hand, it is the work of God in our life, and on the other, our commitment to follow and honour Christ. But of course, this involves the cross.

Restoring the image

God has not given up on his world. He has not given up on us. He took the initiative to close the gap between us, by restoring the broken relationship that results from our sinfulness. He also set about restoring the broken image, the image of God in every human, which is spoiled and shattered by the damaging effects of sin. When God, by his Spirit, opens our eyes to see what he has done, our minds to understand the implications for our lives, and our hearts to respond, there is a recreative act of the power of God in our lives. He makes us new and gives us a fresh start. We have a new attitude (wanting to please Christ, not just ourselves), a new goal (to be like him) and a new purpose (to live for him). We are made new. We still have our old sinful nature, but now we are a new creation (2 Corinthians 5:17). Paul put it like this: 'For God, who said, "Let light shine out of darkness," made his light shine in our hearts to give us the light of the knowledge of God's glory displayed in the face of Christ' (2 Corinthians 4:6). Notice how Paul links the original creative act of God with his recreative power in our lives. John Chrysostom, the fourth-century Bishop of Alexandria, saw the miracle of this recreation or 'new creation' as being even greater than the original act. He wrote, 'Then indeed He said, "Let it be, and it was", but now he said nothing, but Himself became Light for us.'[5]

Although you are a new creature, forgiven and justified in the eyes of God, you have the same body, the same personality, the same human nature. But you also have God at work, changing you from the inside. It is not a case of battling on alone to an impossible and unachievable goal. God's Spirit is at work in you to achieve that which, in your best moments at least, you actually long for: to be a better person – to be like Jesus. The Holy Spirit gradually transforms fallible, sinful, human character into the likeness of Jesus. He closes the gap between us.

God's recreative work in restoring his image in us is depicted in various ways in the Bible. God is like a potter remoulding the clay. With a little pressure here and a touch there, he remoulds the misshapen lump of clay into a beautiful vase (Romans 9:21; 2 Corinthians 4:6–9). He is also like a refiner, heating up the molten gold, skimming off the dross from the surface, purifying it and getting rid of the rubbish and impurities from our life, sometimes painfully (1 Peter 1:7).

This process takes a lifetime and, because of our natural sinfulness, it will never be perfected in this life. So we have to say to those who see our obvious flaws and weaknesses, 'Be patient, God is not finished with me yet.' As our bodies get older and less attractive, God continues his work in us, changing our motives, attitudes and behaviour to close the gap between his character and ours. That is why many elderly people with bent and crinkled bodies shine with an inward strength and joy that is truly divine. As Paul wrote, 'Though outwardly we are wasting away, yet inwardly we are being renewed day by day' (2 Corinthians 4:16).

God has shown himself to be both Creator and Restorer. Whenever we see creativity and restoration, rather than destruction, in our world, we see the character of God being expressed, and God at work closing the gaps.

We all know what human nature is like. We see it all too clearly in ourselves in our less attractive moments. We see the awful results of its expression in the breakdown of marriages, families and societies. But whenever we see people changing, becoming less selfish, more faithful, more patient, showing greater self-control in the face of provocation and temptation, we see and experience God at work by his Spirit in the world. When our children were growing up, my wife would speak to me from time to time about seeing 'signs of grace' in them. When we saw them showing the fruit of the Spirit (Galatians 5:22), rather than their natural sinfulness, then we would be thankful. We could see God at work in their lives for good.

The apostle Paul describes the gradual process of trans-formation that is God's plan for our life in these words: 'We . . . are being transformed into his image with ever-increasing glory, which comes from the Lord, who is the Spirit' (2 Corinthians 3:18). In this same letter, Paul had previously referred back to the time when Moses had come down from Mount Sinai with God's commandments (verses 13–15). According to the account in the Old Testament book of Exodus, Moses' face was shining with the glory of God as he came down the mountain, *but he was not aware of it*. There is a great truth here. When people are truly Christ-like, they may not necessarily be aware of it, but those who are blessed by their lives are.

Make every effort . . .

The process of change is not just one we leave totally to God. Even though the Bible makes clear that salvation is the work of God and not earned by our own effort, it is equally clear that, once we have come to know God, we are called to cooperate with him in his intent to change us for the better. The apostle Peter explains this balance between the work of God in us, and our responsibility, with these words:

> His divine power has given us everything we need for a godly life through our knowledge of him who called us by his own glory and goodness. Through these he has given us his very great and precious promises, so that through them you may participate in the divine nature, having escaped the corruption in the world caused by evil desires.
> (2 Peter 1:3–4)

He goes on:

> For this very reason, *make every effort* to add to your faith goodness; and to goodness, knowledge; and to knowledge, self-control; and to self-control, perseverance; and to perseverance, godliness; and to godliness, mutual affection; and to mutual affection, love.
> (verses 5–7, italics mine)

Here is Peter's version of the fruit of the Spirit or, to put it another way, the characteristics of a godly life. Is there a contradiction here? On the one hand, our character is transformed by the work of the Holy Spirit. On the other hand, we are to make every effort to change. Which is it?

The Bible's answer is both. We cannot change ourselves by self-effort alone, however many New Year's resolutions we make. But when we become Christians, we are promised all the help and enabling of 'his divine power' and all the encouragement of 'his very great and precious promises'.

In the words of John Bunyan,

Run, John, run, the law commands
But gives us neither feet nor hands,
Far better news the gospel brings:
It bids us fly and gives us wings.[6]

Change, difficulty and suffering

Any experience of suffering can leave us asking, 'Why?'. Why did it happen? Why did it happen *to me*? Why did God allow it? In this life we may never receive answers to those questions, but one thing we can affirm with certainty is the 'inconvenient truth' that God often uses our experiences of difficulty to change us into the people he wants us to be.

It is also true that we often come to know God better and experience his power more in times of pressure, and even suffering, than in the good times. It is one thing to believe in God and profess that belief when life is easy; it is quite another to keep trusting when events seem to turn against us. As every Christian knows, and as the Bible makes very clear, the peace and joy promised in the gospel are often mixed inextricably with difficulty and suffering. If we don't accept that, we are blinding our eyes to much of the New Testament. If we do not deal with it in our churches, we are creating an unreal expectation about Christian experience. The temptation for us always to focus on the comforting parts of the Bible, and to avoid the disturbing passages, is one we have to resist. To be honest Christians we must deal with both. We will come back to this issue later in this book.

My wife suffered from a twisted bowel while we were living in Papua New Guinea. She had to wait in the hospital for six hours in unbearable pain, as the only available surgeon was operating on a car-crash victim. By the time the doctor finally cut out a large piece of gangrenous bowel, the situation had become life-threatening. It was in that experience, and while reflecting on it in recovery, that she experienced God very close. Later she shared with me that she now *understood* what it meant to 'Consider it pure joy, my brothers and sisters, whenever you face trials of many kinds, because you know that the testing of your faith produces perseverance' (James 1:2–3); and that she *knew* God had allowed it to happen because he loved her. In the wisdom of God, her life-threatening experience became also a life-changing experience.

When trouble hits us, we would much rather soar above the turbulence than fly through it. While we may pray to God to lift us up and out of our troubles, he sometimes calls us to battle through them.

Certainly that was Paul's experience. Paul had healed others and had experienced God's supernatural power on many occasions. But, through an ordeal of physical pain, he was also called to learn a different lesson: namely that God's grace was enough to see him through and that God's strength is made perfect in human weakness (2 Corinthians 12:9).

He learned from hard experience that, 'when I am weak, then I am strong' (12:10). This is one of a number of biblical paradoxes which reveal a deep truth. When we think we are strong, then we tend to rely wholly on ourselves, and we are, at that moment, most weak. Conversely, when we feel desperately weak, such that we have to rely on God, then we are truly strong.

What is meant by 'weakness' here? Clearly not weakness of character, moral weakness, or necessarily even muscular weakness: Paul's journeys in the book of Acts show that he was a courageous man, with great physical endurance. No, he just means 'human-ness': all that goes with having a human body which is fundamentally weak and vulnerable.

When we forget the true extent of this vulnerability, we may receive sharp reminders. Inwardly, a tiny virus can cause even a strong human body to waste away. Outwardly, our bodies are easily damaged. A friend of mine was a very successful international yachtsman. One day he stepped into the road by mistake and was hit by a car. After weeks of intensive care, he gradually recovered, but only partially. His brain will never function fully again.

Visit an old people's home and see rich, intelligent, athletic men and women reduced to total dependence and confined to a bed or wheelchair. This is what Paul means by weakness. He makes this clear in the same letter to the Corinthians. When writing about enjoyment of the life-changing power of God, he adds this qualification: 'But we have this treasure in jars of clay' (2 Corinthians 4:7), in human bodies that are subject to decay and death. It is in this same second letter to the Corinthians, in which he writes extensively about the power of God and his spiritual highs (12:1–3), that he also tells of his experiences of unrelenting pressure, unrelieved discomfort and (seemingly) unanswered prayer, and insists that God's grace is sufficient to bring him through any difficulty. He had learned that God's power is made perfect in weakness.

Under pressure

Looking back over his years of travel as a missionary, Paul writes, 'We were under great pressure, far beyond our ability to endure, so that we despaired of life itself' (2 Corinthians 1:8). As Paul looked back on this experience of personal danger, he remembers, ' . . . this happened that we might not rely on ourselves but on God, who raises the dead' (1:9). He had learned to rely totally on God in a situation where there was nowhere else to turn.

Paul is not just writing about the triumph of the human spirit over adversity, like the inspiring stories of mountaineers, yachtsmen or explorers surviving against all the odds. Rather, he is speaking of an experience of God, who had so worked in his life that he came through this dark time with a stronger faith and a thankful heart. Later in this letter, he gives us another insight into his need for God's strength just to survive, just to keep going. Unburdening his soul, he writes that he was 'hard pressed . . . perplexed . . . persecuted . . . struck down, but . . . '. 'But' is a powerful word and Paul uses it to describe a powerful experience. He was 'hard pressed, *but* not crushed; perplexed, *but* not in despair; persecuted, *but* not abandoned; struck down, *but* not destroyed' (4:9, italics mine). Paul knew that his experiences of God's power, taken together with his experiences of human weakness, were both a reminder and a demonstration that 'this all-surpassing power is from God and not from us' (4:7).

This letter sets out a truth that is contrary to our natural thinking. The power of God is usually seen not in people who are powerful in human terms: not in high-profile leaders, nor necessarily in the attractive, forceful, assertive, confident, successful ones, but rather in all those whose hope is in God.

It is also clear that God uses experiences of difficulty, and even suffering, to change us.

When you squeeze an orange, applying pressure from the outside, what comes out is what is inside. Similarly, when pressure is applied to our lives, physical, emotional or mental, what comes out is what is inside. Under pressure, we may quickly get irritable or angry, and become full of self-pity. We may say and do things that we later regret. But if we are truly full of the Holy Spirit, as many Christians claim to be, then what comes out under pressure will be the godly qualities of love, joy, peace and patience. The true quality of our Christian life is measured not by what we say, or by what gifts we have; not by how long we have been a Christian, or by the position we hold in the church. It is measured by how we respond under pressure.

As a young married couple living in Mauritius, my wife and I became friends with an older lady who held down a full-time job, while at the same time nursing a close friend at home, who in old age had become extremely difficult and demanding. Furthermore, our friend somehow found time to help out at a children's home, to chair the local Bible Society and found a branch of Scripture Union. On her table she kept a card printed with this verse:

Pressed by the sorrows that each day brings
Pressed into faith for impossible things
Pressed into looking each day to the Lord
Pressed into living a Christ-life outpoured.[7]

It is often in such times of pressure, when we may feel that God is far away, that he works through us, and that others see him at work in us, changing us for good. Certainly, when I think of Christ-like people I have known, this lady comes to mind, although she would probably have been quite amazed to know that.

It is all too easy to be glib in talking or writing about suffering when we are not going through it ourselves. I am in awe of those who have suffered imprisonment, torture and death for no crime at all, or those who have spent their whole lives in physical pain because of an ailment or disability, or have struggled for years, often with little support, caring for a family member with a disability or dementia.

As with all things in the Christian life, the best example to look to is Jesus himself. In the Gospels we see him tired and worn out, yet still giving time to others. On the night before his death, with the terrible burden of that on his soul, he was still caring most about the needs of others. Even in the agony of death, we see him praying for his enemies and caring for his mother. What came out of Jesus, when under extreme pressure, was pure gold in terms of human character.

As we have already seen, we may not always get answers from God when we ask, 'Why?' What we can say with certainty, however, is that any difficulty and suffering in life provides a new opportunity to change, through experiencing God who, in Christ, knew what it was to suffer. Indeed, the Bible speaks of 'participation in his [Christ's] sufferings' (Philippians 3:10).

The cross

Whether or not God takes us down the path of difficulty, we will most certainly face hurt to our pride and ego as he works on our selfish nature. If our character is to change and become more Christ-like, then we need to take seriously these words of Jesus: 'Whoever wants to be my disciple must deny themselves and take up their cross and follow me' (Mark 8:34).

Paul's New Testament letters have the same message. For example, he writes to the Colossians, 'Put to death, therefore, whatever belongs to your earthly nature' (3:5), by which, he explains, he is referring to sexual immorality, greed, anger, rage, malice, slander, filthy language and lying.

As the late Festo Kivengere (former Bishop of Uganda) used to say, 'The cross must cross you!' After all, if the Spirit of Jesus is really in us, then it is the Spirit of one who died and rose again. Therefore, if we want to experience his resurrection power, it will certainly also involve an experience of the cross, a painful battle with our human nature which always wants to assert itself.

Picture yourself for a moment in a situation of conflict with your spouse or closest friend. You may be having a full-on argument. Or you may each have withdrawn into your respective corners for a protracted sulk. Either way, there will be a crucial moment when you become very aware of a choice. You can either assert yourself ever more strongly and inflict more pain in the form of hurtful words (or worse) on someone you claim to love. Or you can deny yourself, face up to your sin in all its ugliness, and apologize and seek the help of the Holy Spirit to restore your peace and restore the relationship. You face the clear choice of making the first move to reconciliation *now*, or doing nothing and waiting for the other person to take the first step.

In the words of Paul (Romans 6), in such situations either we yield ourselves to sin as a controlling power, or we yield ourselves to God. There is a battle for control of your life between your sinful nature and the Holy Spirit. The more we choose the latter path in the multitude of such situations in which we find ourselves each day, the more we become like Christ, and the more the gap between what we say we believe and how we behave is closed.

Reflection

The life of someone who is truly filled with the Spirit, in whom God is working to restore his broken image, a person who is committed to change and is battling through the daily conflict with sin and self, is a life which is *worthy*: a life in which the gap between belief and behaviour is gradually being closed.

What does it mean to live a life *worthy of our calling* (Ephesians 4:1)?

What does it mean to live a life *worthy of the gospel* (Philippians 1:27)?

What does it mean to treat others in a manner *worthy of God* (3 John 6)?

4. Growing relationships

*Dad was a great talent, a remarkable man who stood
for peace and love in the world. But at the same time he
found it very hard to show any peace and love
to his first family – my mother and me.*
Julian Lennon[1]

The gap between the quality of our relationships and how God intends them to be

Julian Lennon's comment about his famous father John could be said of many of us. There is a gap between what we say we stand for and how we behave. It's easy to advocate world peace – much harder to make peace with your spouse, your workmate or your neighbour.

In his book *Mere Christianity*, C. S. Lewis tries to get us to focus on the personal and the practical, rather than on the conceptual and general, in the matter of forgiveness. He wrote these words in the context of post-war debate among intellectuals about whether the Nazis could ever be forgiven for their war crimes:

> When you start mathematics you do not begin with the
> calculus; you begin with simple addition. In the same way, if we
> want (but all depends on wanting) to learn to forgive, perhaps
> we had better start with something easier than the Gestapo. One

might start with forgiving one's husband or wife, or parents or children . . . That will probably keep us busy for the moment.[2]

God's opportunities for us to live out our faith are always *here and now*, with real people, in our day-to-day relationships. God calls us to work with what we've got, in the situations in which he has placed us. To put it in secular terms, you have to play the cards you are dealt.

John Smith, the Australian evangelist, once said that to be disillusioned one must first be living an illusion. In the Bible, God seems to be very concerned about the illusion that many people are living under, about the real state of their professed relationship with him, given the quality of their relationships with other people.

The Bible is consistently, and ruthlessly, honest and confronting about this matter of our relationships with other people. In his first letter, written to professing Christians whose lives obviously manifested a lot of gaps and inconsistencies, the apostle John writes, 'Whoever claims to love God yet hates a brother or sister is a liar. For whoever does not love their brother or sister, whom they have seen, cannot love God, whom they have not seen . . . anyone who loves God must also love their brother and sister' (1 John 4:20–21). And again, 'Anyone who claims to be in the light but hates a brother or sister is still in the darkness' (1 John 2:9).

With relentless logic, John exposes the gap between what we may *claim* in terms of our relationship with God on the one hand, and the quality of our interpersonal relationships on the other. If you have hatred in your heart, you cannot be in fellowship with God, whatever you profess to believe and whatever your religious experience. If you cannot love another human being whom you can talk to, apologize to and care for, how can you claim to love God whose nature is love, whom you have not seen (1 John 4:7, 12)? The Bible does not allow us the luxury of the hypocrisy (for that is ultimately what it is) of divorcing our religious faith from our relationships with other people.

Valuing relationships

Love is the environment in which we were created to live. Relationships of love give meaning to life. A friend of mine told how he felt when he visited his eighteen-year-old daughter in hospital after she had been badly injured in a car crash. Her father had only recently bought her the car, which was now a write-off. 'As I sat by her bedside,' said my friend, 'praying for her recovery, I never gave the car a thought.' Of course! It's not *things* that give meaning to life; it's *relationships*.

I have in front of me a newspaper article about the terrible Australian bushfires of 2009, in which 173 people died and many more lost their homes. Attached to the article is a photo of a young couple, standing in the ruins of their dream home in the Victorian bush, in close embrace. The writer describes their 'realisation that while they may have lost everything else, all they have left in the world is each other and that really does mean the whole world'. One reader then adds her comment on the tragedy: 'This is a wake-up call to tell your family you love them. Hold them close. Who knows what tomorrow brings?'[3]

The Bible majors on relationships. In his prayer in John's Gospel, Jesus refers to eternal life in terms of a relationship: 'Now this is eternal life: that they know you, the only true God, and Jesus Christ, whom you have sent' (John 17:3). Eternal life is to be in right relationship with God forever.

The Bible makes clear, however, that we can enjoy that relationship with God only when we are in right relationship with others, and that our relationship with God is to be reflected in those relationships.

I have heard stressed-out teachers say (half-jokingly perhaps), 'We could have a great school here if it weren't for the students.' Under the pressure and frustrations of hospital administration, I have known doctors and nurses express similar sentiments about their patients!

There is a danger that we might find ourselves thinking the same way in terms of our relationship with God. Picture yourself coming back from a great worship service or from enjoying God's creation. You feel at peace with God and with the world; you might believe in such moments that you have finally got the Christian life sorted out. Then . . . down to earth. You return to your flat and find everyone has left *you* to wash the dishes, or you end up getting into a silly argument with a family member about which TV programme to watch, or you go back to work and find people being unreasonably demanding. At such times, you might (like me!) be tempted to think, 'I could be really holy if only it weren't for all the people I have to deal with!'

But, of course, that would be to miss the point completely. It is in our relationships that our faith has to be lived out and our love expressed. In the Bible, God gives us the model for that love on which all our relationships are to be based. Faithful, sacrificial, selfless love is the paradigm.

Perhaps the most beautiful word in the Old Testament is the Hebrew word transliterated *chesedh*, frequently used to describe the love of God for his people. However, it loses much in translation. No single English word can bring out the richness of its meaning. It is variously translated in our English Bibles as steadfast love, unfailing love, devotion, mercy, loving-kindness or constant love. It is a covenant word with a heavy emphasis on loyalty and faithfulness, and it is used, for example, in the chorus in Psalm 118:

> Give thanks to the LORD, for he is good;
>   his love [his steadfast love = *chesedh*] endures for ever.

We praise God for his greatness and holiness, and for what he has done. But note that here it is God's steadfast, faithful love for us that is at the core of our relationship with him, which provides the reason for us to praise him.

When that sort of love, the love of God, is being shown in our friendships, our family and our marriage, then our lives become more aligned with our professed beliefs. A gap is closed.

Friendship

The gift of friendship is not the exclusive property of Christians. It is part of God's common grace to all his creatures. Faithful friendships enrich our lives. We are not meant to live in isolation from one another; nor are we meant to limit our friendships to fellow Christians.

Caring friendships are central to our humanity. Sharon Commins, the Irish aid worker who was held hostage in Sudan for several months in 2010, said she would have died, but for the emotional and practical support of her fellow captive, Hilda Kawuki. Commenting on this in a newspaper article, Brian Keenan, who had himself been held hostage in Beirut from 1986 to 1990, wrote, 'By making and acknowledging that commitment with another "being" our humanity is assured.'[4]

But caring friendships are also central to Christian faith. Abraham is described in the Bible as 'God's friend' (James 2:23). God's covenant with Abraham, which is foundational to all that follows in the Bible, is expressed in terms of covenant friendship: that is, faithful, constant, loving friendship. Jesus assured his disciples that, as trusting, obedient followers, they were also his friends, for whom he would lay down his life (John 15:13, 14).

Human friendship at its best, when two people support each other in triumph or adversity, is a reflection of God's friendship with us. The Bible gives us several examples of how this is worked out in practice.

David and Jonathan made a covenant of friendship with each other. We see how powerful this was, even many years after Jonathan's death. David had finally become king of Israel and, in the warring climate of the time, he was expected to wipe out the families of his enemies, especially those related to the former king, Saul, who had tried repeatedly to kill him. But David asked, 'Is there anyone still left of the house of Saul to whom I can show kindness [*chesedh*] for Jonathan's sake?' (2 Samuel 9:1). There was someone left: Jonathan's son Mephibosheth, who was lame. In front of the royal court, David promised him, 'I will surely show you kindness for the sake of your father Jonathan' (9:7).

David knew the covenant love of God himself and showed that same love to his best friend's needy son. He wrote many poems and songs about God's covenant love, including the famous 'Shepherd Psalm', in which he joyfully and confidently asserts,

> Surely your goodness and love [*chesedh*] will follow me
>> all the days of my life.
> (Psalm 23:6)

We find a second example of covenant friendship in David's life, in his faithful leadership of the band of men who supported him in his difficult years, when he was a fugitive from King Saul. On one occasion, when David must have been worn out and depressed from having to live constantly on the run, and was longing to be back in his home town (Bethlehem), he cried out, 'Oh, that someone would get me a drink of water from the well near the gate of Bethlehem!' (2 Samuel 23:15). Some of David's men overheard him and went out, crossed enemy lines and, at great risk to their own lives, brought him back a flask of water from Bethlehem. David responded in a seemingly strange way. He poured it on the ground.

Was he spurning the gift his men had brought him? No! The Bible does not say that he poured it *away*, but that 'he poured it out before the LORD' (v. 16). He offered it as a drink offering to God. He had so much respect for what his men had done for him, that he did not feel worthy to drink it. Instead, he offered it to the Lord.

In this story we see the chain of God's covenant love working out in human relationships. Because David knew the love of God, he could express it to others. His covenant love for his men inspired them to risk their lives for him. He, in turn, honoured that commitment and showed his respect for his men, by offering their love gift back to God.

It is because David sought to express the love he had received from God in his dealings with others that, despite all his many public and major moral failures, he could still be called 'a man after [God's] own heart' (Acts 13:22).

We see the same sort of covenant faithfulness in the relationship between Ruth and her aged mother-in-law Naomi. Naomi was concerned that Ruth's devotion to her would limit her opportunity of marriage, and therefore (in that society, at that time) her opportunity of security, financial support and loving care. Naomi encouraged Ruth to leave her and find a husband (Ruth 1:8–13). But Ruth was a woman of God and she committed herself to stick with Naomi, with these words: 'Where you go I will go, and where you stay I will stay' (1:16). Later, in God's providence, Ruth found a husband, Boaz, who was a good man. So God honoured Ruth's faithful love to Naomi, the covenant love which reflected God's love for her, and which she then showed in her dealings with others.

If our faith and hope are real, if the Holy Spirit is truly at work in our lives, then that will be expressed in our friendships. People will see something of Christ in how we treat people, something of the covenant friendship in which God relates to his people. There will be no credibility gap between what we claim to believe and how we relate to others.

Family life

Single or married, our Christian faith will be tested most severely at home and at work. We will look at the latter in the next chapter, but let's think for a moment about our family situation.

Family life, in all its shapes, is a real proving ground for exercising Christian love and all the other fruits of the Holy Spirit. If a Christian is truly full of the Holy Spirit, then the change will be evident in the home. Parents will see it in their children and vice versa.

It is with our parents, our children, our siblings, grandparents and our in-laws that we find the practical opportunities every day to exercise love, patience, long-suffering and selfless care. It is in the home that we are called on to give time and energy to demanding sick relatives, grouchy parents or delinquent children. In the home we will find opportunities to show loving care and wisdom when we have to deal with marriage breakdown, abuse, dementia and all the other results of sinful human nature that damage relationships and stretch us to breaking point.

In the home, God calls us to develop relationships of love that stand the test of time. That requires us each day to learn to give and to forgive: to *give* as Christ gave himself for us and to *forgive* as God, in Christ, has forgiven us. We are to keep short accounts with one another and with God. We are not to 'let the sun go down while [we] are still angry' (Ephesians 4:26).

Ever since the garden of Eden, it has come quite naturally to human beings to blame someone else when things go wrong. Children learn to play the blame game from a very early age. 'Sorry is the hardest word' to say and sometimes the hardest word to mean, even within a family. But it is always the crucial first step in restoring damaged relationships. Think for a moment. When did words such as, 'It was *my* fault; I am to blame' last pass your lips in talking to your spouse, your children, your parents or your brothers and sisters?

A work colleague once summed up his philosophy about relationships like this: 'I'll meet anyone halfway – no further.' Some families try to operate like that. By contrast, living out the Christian life in the home means always being the first to make the move, to humble ourselves and to go *the whole way* to restore and maintain the relationship, and not to wait for the other person to apologize. Jesus did not meet us halfway to restore our broken relationship with God. He went all the way to the cross, and we are called to follow in his footsteps.

Strong families show *chesedh* every day in relating to one another, and parents are called to set that example to their children.

Love and marriage

A loving marriage relationship is a living example of the spiritual relationship between us and the Lord Jesus Christ. Indeed, it is not so much that the relationship between Christ and the believer can be likened to a marriage relationship, but rather the other way round, that the marriage relationship is modelled on the relationship between Christ and his people. As the apostle Paul wrote, 'A man will leave his father and mother and be united to his wife, and the two will become one flesh. This is a profound mystery – but I am talking about Christ and the church' (Ephesians 5:31–32). When Paul pictures the way a man should love his wife, he uses Christ's love for us as his model: 'Husbands, love your wives, *just as Christ loved the church* and gave himself up for her' (Ephesians 5:25, italics mine).

We also find this marriage analogy in the writings of the Old Testament prophets (see, for example, the books of Jeremiah and Hosea), where the relationship between God and Israel is likened to that between a man and a woman and, specifically, between a faithful husband and a faithless wife. Hosea married a woman who was unfaithful and turned away from him to prostitution. God commanded Hosea to take the initiative to forgive and restore that relationship: 'Go, show your love to your wife again . . . Love her *as the LORD loves the Israelites*' (Hosea 3:1, italics mine).

What is a marriage relationship like that shows this sort of love? First, it is full of *forgiveness*. We are called to forgive 'just as in Christ God forgave you' (Ephesians 4:32). Notice that this command, which also appears in the Lord's Prayer, is to model our relationships with other people on God's love for us.

Second, it is a *caring* relationship: as God cares for us, so we are to care for one another, as in the words of the marriage service in the 1662 Anglican Book of Common Prayer: 'for better, for worse, for richer, for poorer, in sickness and in health'. When we are tired and discouraged, in pain or under great stress, we all appreciate some TLC (Tender Loving Care). So we are called to follow Christ's example and give it to others.

Third, it is a *self-giving* love. We are to love like Christ, who gave himself for us. We are to spend ourselves in service of one another, a call that cuts right across our natural selfishness and self-centredness. Marriage teaches us a lot about unselfishness: it was only after I got married that I realized how innately selfish I was. Most men will not be called on to die for their wives, but every Christian husband is called to give his life, in the sense of putting his wife first, devoting time, energy, a listening ear and practical and emotional support. Wives in Christian marriages have a similar high calling (Ephesians 5:22), in terms of submission to their husbands. The respective commands to husbands and wives are really two sides of the same coin: both require marriage partners to put the other first. The call to both is to 'Submit to one another out of reverence for Christ' (Ephesians 5:21).

It is also *a love which respects the other*. Marriages start to fall apart when one party no longer treats the other with respect, but takes their partner for granted; when a man treats other women with more respect than he does his own wife, or when a woman 'rubbishes' her husband behind his back in conversation with her friends.

Marriage relationships also run into trouble when one partner tries to dominate the other. God does not 'steamroller' our personality in that way. Rather, he works to bring our gifts, talents and qualities to full flower. So we are to respect one another's gifts, abilities and opinions. Relationships flourish when we encourage one another, not when we put one another down. One man said that his wife's encouragement was like 'the wind in his sails' that kept him moving in the right direction. I love that description.

Fundamentally, it is a love founded on *total commitment*. Christ gave himself totally for us: 'Having loved his own who were in the world, [Jesus] loved them to the end' (John 13:1).

When two people get married, it means total commitment. In many cultures today there seems to be much greater effort put into preparing for the *wedding* than preparing for the *marriage*. Unaffordable amounts of money, months of preparation, long shopping trips and many tears are spent in preparation for the great day.

With so many marriages ending in separation and divorce, we must wonder why a similar effort is not put into preparing a man and a woman for the marriage, which is intended to last for a lifetime.

When a man and a woman commit themselves in Christian marriage, it means that, from that day forward, each puts the other first, before family and friends. When you marry, your number one commitment in human terms is now to your partner. You belong to each other; the two have become one. This means that you don't give up loving when the relationship hits a few problems. Rather, commitment provides the framework within which love can work through the problems. Certainly, there may be exceptional circumstances – desertion, or physical and mental abuse – when the relationship cannot be restored. However, such exceptions serve to prove the rule, which is that marriage love, modelled on God's love, is constant. Jesus said, 'Never will I leave you; never will I forsake you' (Hebrews 13:5). So we always need to 'be there for each other'.

Forgiveness, caring, self-giving, respect and commitment – these are the characteristics of covenant love, the love God has for us, the love Christ has showed us and continues to show to us. Whenever we see this type of love in a marriage, or in any human relationship, we see the character of God being lived out, and we experience his reality here and now.

The late W. E. Sangster, a Methodist preacher who ministered in London in the 1940s and '50s, as he was dying, told his son, 'Son, I've never been more sure in my life of the two things that matter to me – the truth of our religion and the love of your mother.'[5] What a great way to die, full of assurance about relationships that truly matter!

A life of love

My job has involved a lot of travelling, a lot of time at airports. I find myself watching people greet one another. You can see pure happiness in so many faces – as two lovers meet after a separation, or a grandmother sees her infant grandchild for the first time, or as children run into the arms of a parent who has been away. Love is much more than the warm feeling of being reunited or reconciled. But every time we see love shown and love in action, we glimpse something of the character of God, and we see life as it was always meant to be.

'Keep yourselves in God's love,' says Jude in his New Testament letter (verse 21). What does that mean? It means to *enjoy* the great privilege of having a relationship with God through Jesus Christ; to live each day reminding yourself that God loves you, that you are 'accepted in the Beloved' (Ephesians 1:6 NKJV). You are in a covenant relationship of love, in a secure relationship which goes on beyond the grave. To 'keep yourself in the love of God' is to live in the light rather than in the dark, to live in the warmth of the sun rather than out in the cold. It is a wonderful thing to know that you are loved. Many of us feel so unlovable much of the time, which is why we have such difficulty accepting the grace of God and grasping the truth that God loves and accepts us *as we are*.

To keep ourselves in the love of God also means that we are to go out each day to reflect that love in our relationships with others. 'Live a life of love, just as Christ loved us' is Paul's call in Ephesians (5:2). To show *love* instead of bitterness and resentment is to bring others out into the warmth. It is a wonderful thing to give love.

To hurt and fight and betray, to suffer the pain that comes with the breakdown of a relationship, is to experience a foretaste of hell on earth. The converse is also true. Reconciliation after a dispute or an argument is to experience a foretaste of heaven on earth. Picture a situation where two friends have argued and are not speaking to each other. One softens and apologizes. There is restoration, a warm embrace, perhaps tears. The old proverb says that 'to err is human; to forgive divine'. When a broken relationship is restored, there is an experience *now* of heaven, when restoration and reconciliation will be perfect and complete.

On one occasion when we had a large group of friends at our home, I looked across the room and noticed that at either end were two men, both Christian leaders, who had fallen out and were not speaking to each other. How they managed to reconcile that with their conscience before God I don't know. I asked myself the question: What would it take for one man to cross the room, apologize to the other, put things right and shake hands and embrace? The only answer that occurred to me was the same power that brought Jesus out of the tomb. If you think I am overstating the problem, read Paul's prayer for the Ephesians, recorded in his letter. There he prays, 'that you may know . . . his incomparably great power . . . That power is the same as the mighty strength he exerted when he raised Christ from the dead' (Ephesians 1:18–20). The power of God at work in the Christian is resurrection power. That power, in God's plan, is given to enable us to do things that our natural selfishness or weakness would not lead us to do, and to be people that our natural sinfulness would prevent us from becoming. The grace that is seen in reconciling broken relationships, in going the extra mile, in being the first to move to put things right, is truly resurrection power. Whenever we see it in action, we see the living God at work to close the gaps.

On one occasion at work, I was having a problem with an employee. It was the time of the annual performance review, and I came home feeling that this person was not supporting me enough, but I also had a nagging feeling that I could have handled the situation better. Sitting in church that Sunday, I could not concentrate on worship. I was very troubled and convicted about *my* attitude and *my* behaviour. Reflecting on the views expressed to me forcibly by my unhappy employee, I found myself thinking that he had made several good points, that I had not given a fair or balanced appraisal. As I prayed about that relationship, I had been mentally picturing that the person would either resign or apologize to me. But leaving the church that day, I knew that *I* had to repair the relationship. Back at work on Monday, I apologized and we moved on. God answered my prayer for improvement in the relationship, but not in the way I had originally envisaged.

We cannot go on separating our relationship with God from our relationships with those God has given us to live and work with. Perhaps there is an apology you need to offer, a phone call to make, an email to send to put things right with someone before you next go to worship God. Perhaps you need to learn to value people more, to invest more of your time in relationships, to recover a sense of those things that really matter.

Jesus told his disciples, '*As I have loved you*, so you must love one another' (John 13:34, italics mine). Whenever we show the sort of self-sacrificing constant love that Jesus shows to us, in marriage, friendships, family or any other relationship, then we experience a foretaste of heaven on earth, of the gap being closed.

Reflection

Read Ephesians 5.

What do you need to put right with God that is a barrier to a deeper relationship with him (1 John 1:5–10)?

What relationships are most important to your life?

What relationships do you need to put right?

What actions do you need to take right now (see, for example, Matthew 5:23–24)?

PART 3:
THE GAP IS CLOSED . . .
WHEN WE MAKE A DIFFERENCE

5. Working it out

We must have a seven-days' religion,
or else we have none at all.
Periodical godliness is perpetual hypocrisy.
C. H. Spurgeon[1]

The gap between what I say I believe and how I behave at work

I am continually challenged by what it means to be a Christian in the workplace. It is a most depressing thing to hear a non-Christian say at work (as I have heard about a number of people), 'That guy calls himself a Christian. I think he's a leader in his church, but you would never believe it from the way he does business, the way he talks and the way he treats people.' His local church may regard the person in question as a strong leader who gets things done. But those who encounter him in business negotiations may see him as a bully who treads on people to get his own way.

The biggest battle most of us face is how to live out our Christian life at work. Not just by being ethically honest, but in the way we handle office politics, the way we treat others. When I first came to the Middle East, a friend half-jokingly advised me that the way to succeed was: 'Kiss up and kick down.' Yet, as Christians, we are called to 'Support up and care down'. My behaviour and words under stress, the encouragement I give, or lack of it, my integrity – these are what leave a lasting impression.

How we live day by day, hour by hour, is meant to be as much an act of worship, of honouring God, as our time at church, and a witness, spoken or unspoken, to what we believe about God. Nowhere is this challenge to live a consistently whole life greater than at work. It is at work that we interact with non-Christian people, where we grapple with interpersonal relationships under pressure, with moral and ethical issues, and often when we are physically and mentally tired.

By work, I mean not only paid employment, but any work we do, including homemaking, voluntary work or study. All are opportunities for worship and witness. Work is effort directed towards an end, whether it's washing the dishes, running a company, laying bricks or writing an essay. Work can be cerebral, manual or full-body activity.

One person's work can be another person's play. My late father, who worked in an office all his life, used to enjoy gardening as relaxation. Those who earn their living as gardeners may prefer to sit at a computer in their leisure time!

Some people's work is project-related, like that of a builder, an engineer or a software developer, where there is a definite finished product and the motivation to keep going to complete the job. For others, such as child-care workers, assembly-line operatives, shopkeepers or homemakers, the work is more repetitive. Similar tasks are performed each day. That presents very different challenges.

If we work in a large organization, such as a government bureaucracy, the military or a large corporation, we face, consciously or unconsciously, directly or indirectly, pressure to conform; to become 'another brick in the wall', another cog in the machine. Working for 'the man', whether the bureaucratic machine of government, the military hierarchy or the private corporation, can gradually affect the way we think and act, and lead us to compromise our beliefs and values.

All large organizations demand conformity to their policies, procedures, and sometimes to their dress codes. But they may also demand, subtly or overtly, conformity to moral and ethical standards, and implicit endorsement of values contrary to our own. In the battle to preserve our own values, we can find that we are behaving one way at work, applying one set of values there, and another in our lives outside.

Joel Bakan, Professor of Law at the University of British Columbia, quotes the words of a competitive intelligence expert (a corporate spy) he had interviewed, a man who had learned to compartmentalize his life in order to survive: 'There's so much trickery and deception in my job that I don't really want it in my private life,' he is quoted as saying:

> I can go and pick the pocket of some executive at a trade show in Miami so badly that I know his company's going out of business in six months and I can go home and sleep like a baby, and it's no big deal, you know, because it's business . . . The way you live with yourself is to have a very compartmentalized life.[2]

Bakan observes that this intelligence expert believed he was a decent person because he could draw a line between his corporate and his personal life.

We may recoil from such an honest confession, but let's not deceive ourselves. Perhaps Bakan's example is just an acute case of a common disease, the mistaken desire to make life easier for ourselves. Ask yourself, do you sleep easier at night by keeping your 'work life' nicely separated from your profession of Christian faith? Whatever our work environment, it is all too easy to live a very compartmentalized life, for there to be a big gap between our values in the workplace and those we apply outside.

The Christian gospel changes people's lives, and therefore it must change our attitude to work. Every Christian has to face the question: 'How does my faith impact on my work?' In a seventy-five-year lifespan, we might typically spend twenty-five years asleep (what a thought!), another twenty years shopping, eating, playing sport or relaxing, which leaves us at least twenty-five or thirty years working. So it's hard to say you are living a Christian life if more than half your waking hours on earth are not affected by your faith!

The shorter catechism of the Westminster Confession of Faith contains this wonderfully direct statement: 'The chief end of man is to glorify God and to enjoy Him forever.' If the purpose of our life is to glorify God and to enjoy our relation-ship with him, then we need to ask ourselves how we can do that in and through our daily work.

The big challenge for the Christian in any work environ-ment is to maintain personal standards of integrity and, in whatever way the role allows, to be an influence for good, to close the gaps between behaviour at work and behaviour outside, between the faith professed in private and the life lived out in public each day.

Mark Greene, Executive Director of the London Institute for Contemporary Christianity (LICC), has highlighted the 'Sacred-Secular Divide' (SSD) as 'the biggest challenge facing the Christian church in the twenty-first century'.[3] As one who has spent half a lifetime seeking to apply my Christian faith to my life and work, I can relate to that. Indeed, I would add that it is also the biggest challenge facing every Christian, every day. As Mark Greene observes, referring to the SSD, 'It is the malignant foe of fruitful mission and joyful Christian living. There is a better way.' There certainly is.

Some biblical principles

The Bible has a lot to say about work. First of all, according to Scripture, work is good. God himself is a worker. He made the world and then rested. We are made in his image, and he has placed in us both the desire to create and the ability to find satisfaction in what we achieve.

Jesus was a worker, and not just in the sense that he grew up earning a living as a carpenter. When he left home to spend three years as an itinerant teacher and healer, it was hard, exhausting work, as the Gospels make clear.

Second, the Bible lays down the obvious principle that work is needed if we are to eat, and therefore to live. We who live in towns and cities are used to buying our groceries at the local supermarket or corner store, where we exchange credit or cash for food which has been harvested, processed and packaged by others. We are far removed from primary production. I found it a big shock when I first went to work in my mid-teens to calculate how many hours I had to put in, at my meagre pay rate, in order to earn enough to buy even the basic necessities of life. Our lot in this life, if we are of sound mind and body, is to work in order to survive, and to support those who, because of infirmity, age or lack of opportunity, cannot work.

Laziness is condemned:

> Lazy hands make for poverty,
>> but diligent hands bring wealth.
> (Proverbs 10:4)

The New Testament reinforces the truth that idleness is dishonouring to God (see 2 Thessalonians 3:6–15). The apostle Paul set an example of working long and hard, supporting himself in his missionary work in his trade as a tentmaker. His hard work was part of his witness to others. He wrote to the Christians at Thessalonica, 'Surely you remember, brothers and sisters, our toil and hardship; we worked night and day in order not to be a burden to anyone while we preached the gospel of God to you' (1 Thessalonians 2:9).

Third, work can often be tiring and frustrating. It is one of the results of the fall. Way back at the beginning, for the first humans, getting food was simply a matter of walking round the garden and picking what they wanted. After Adam's sin, God said to him and Eve,

> Cursed is the ground because of you;
>> through painful toil you will eat food from it
>> all the days of your life . . .
> By the sweat of your brow
>> you will eat your food
> until you return to the ground.
> (Genesis 3:17, 19)

And this is how it has been ever since. It may not be pleasant, working long hours out in the fields in the hot sun, or in a factory, or teaching delinquent children, or ironing clothes, or dealing with unhappy customers, or stressing out with work and study deadlines. Work is difficult and demands effort and sacrifice.

Fourth, work can sometimes seem pointless. The book of Ecclesiastes asks the question:

> What do people gain from all their labours
>> at which they toil under the sun?
> (Ecclesiastes 1:3)

Like Sisyphus in the Greek myth, condemned endlessly to roll a heavy stone up a hill, only to see it roll down again, it may be hard for us to find much meaning in our daily task. This does not just apply to boring, repetitive or low-paid work. The writer of Ecclesiastes paints a picture of a successful public leader, with great possessions. After a career of monumental achievements, this man sadly concluded,

> Yet when I surveyed all that my hands had done
>   and what I had toiled to achieve,
> everything was meaningless, a chasing after
>   the wind.
> (Ecclesiastes 2:11)

Even the most successful creative work can seem to lack meaning if it is done without reference to God. Most of us ask ourselves at one time or another in our working life, 'Why am I doing this?' or 'Surely there must be more to life than this?' Sadly, we can change jobs, or even move to another country, and still take our core problem with us: if we are trying to find meaning in life without reference to our Creator, then we will be disappointed.

Without God, even our most treasured achievements may seem ultimately pointless when we face death. The chief executive of a global bank retired recently. In a television interview, he was asked what he would most like to be remembered for. His candid reply took the interviewer by surprise. He said, 'I want to be remembered with affection by my children; in this business I'll be forgotten in a week.' He may have been over-modest. But he knew how hard, and often cynically ruthless, is the world of finance and business, in which even great leaders are quickly forgotten.

Fifth, work is not meant to dominate our lives, leaving no time for God or for relationships. If we are in danger of work taking over our lives to the exclusion of all else, or of working longer and harder just to acquire more possessions, then let's heed the warning in Jesus' story about 'the rich fool' (Luke 12) and the uncertainty of life. Let us also heed the challenge of the prophet Isaiah:

> Why spend money on what is not bread,
>> and your labour on what does not satisfy?
> (Isaiah 55:2)

Have we got our priorities right? Are we making time for what is important as well as what is urgent?

Isaiah goes on to remind us that ultimately only God can satisfy our deepest needs:

> Give ear and come to me;
>> listen, that you may live.
> (Isaiah 55:3)

Jesus reaffirms this, saying, 'Man shall not live on bread alone, but on every word that comes from the mouth of God' (Matthew 4:4). We often speak of the importance of work–life balance for our physical health, and of making quality time to enjoy relationships with friends and family. The Bible underlines the even greater importance of setting aside time to honour God (the Sabbath principle), so that we do not fall into the trap of spending all our mental, physical and emotional energy on work. It also emphasizes the principle of honouring God *in and through* our daily work, not just as an activity *outside* of our working week.

Finding meaning and fulfilment

So how can work be redeemed, or sanctified, changed from a boring, pointless, necessary evil, something we *have* to do, into an activity that has purpose and meaning? The Bible gives a number of answers to this question. First and foremost, we need to see work, like life itself, as *a gift from God*: 'A person can do nothing better than to eat and drink and find satisfaction in their own toil. This too, I see, is from the hand of God' (Ecclesiastes 2:24; see also 3:9–13). It is good to put in a hard day at work and to feel we have accomplished something, to taste how God felt after resting from his work of creation and reflecting that it was good. In most jobs, there is usually *something* in the daily grind and routine that gives us a sense of satisfaction.

But what if our work is very repetitive and routine? How then can we find meaning in our work and honour God through it?

This leads us to a second part of the answer to our question. The degree of fulfilment we find in our work depends ultimately on *our attitude to it*. We are called to do our daily work as if we were working for the Lord himself. This is a life-changing and liberating principle.

Paul gave this instruction to slaves in the first century AD. It is hard to think of a less fulfilling job than slavery, where your best is not valued and you have little or no freedom to express creativity, where the hours are long and the bosses are often difficult or cruel. Paul explains what this involves in his letter to the Ephesians. We are to work 'with sincerity of heart, just as you would obey Christ . . . not only to win their [your earthly masters'] favour when their eye is on you . . . Serve wholeheartedly, as if you were serving the Lord, not people' (Ephesians 6:5–7).

Those two words, 'sincerity' and 'wholeheartedly', describe the attitude which will result in our finding meaning and fulfilment in daily work, and thereby closing the gap between how we behave at work and what we profess to believe in church. Sincerity implies integrity and honesty. To be 'wholehearted' is, by definition, the opposite of having the 'divided heart' (Psalm 86:11) we considered in chapter 3. To work 'wholeheartedly' means that all our motives and energies are aligned in one direction: to please God and honour him.

In any sports team, you may find those who play for themselves (the selfish), those who play for the crowd (the flashy) and those who play for the team and the coach. Many sports clubs give awards at the end of a season to honour the most valuable players, and the most improved. Some also have a special coach's award for the best team players. At work too we can be selfish, trying to manipulate people and situations to show ourselves in the best possible light in front of our bosses. We can grab the credit and the limelight in times of success, or we can be a team player, quietly getting on with the job, applying our best for the good of others, because we are working for the Lord, to please him.

This approach to work is also a way to freedom from drudgery. If our work is difficult, tiring or repetitive (and all jobs include some irksome tasks), then we transform the workplace by seeing our work as part of our daily worship, and therefore doing our best because we are doing it for the Lord.

This is particularly liberating if you have a difficult or frustrating boss. A recent survey of firms in Australia identified that the major reason why employees leave a firm is not pay and conditions, but a problem with their immediate supervisor.[4] It's hard going to work every day for someone you do not like or respect, or who doesn't seem to value your contribution. Changing your attitude is the key. Start performing your work as if you were doing it directly for the Lord himself. Then your work is redeemed to become an act of worship and also an act of witness to the existence and character of God.

The value and sanctity of work in the sight of God was one of the great 'discoveries' of the Protestant Reformation. It was Martin Luther who argued, contrary to the teaching of the church of his day, that the Christian life was a total vocation, that all callings were of equal value and that work in the world was an act potentially just as holy as the spiritual disciplines of prayer, worship, study and meditation. These verses by the seventeenth-century English poet George Herbert illustrate this approach to making work an act of worship:

Teach me, my God and King,
In all things thee to see,
And what I do in any thing,
To do it as for thee.

A servant with this clause
Makes drudgery divine:
Who sweeps a room, as for thy laws,
Makes that and th'action fine.[5]

This work ethic was much ridiculed by Marxists in the twentieth century. They argued that it was a tool used by capitalist bosses in order to exploit workers and increase productivity in the workplace. But this criticism simply ignores the stern things the Bible has to say to bosses as well as workers. A supervisor who does his or her work 'as to the Lord' will then treat those in their charge with respect and fairness, with due care and concern for their safety and welfare, and will compensate them with fair wages.

But it's not an easy road for anyone. We live in a world where we naturally focus on our rights and others' responsibilities. Disturbingly, the Bible turns this around and calls us to concentrate on the rights of others and our responsibilities.

Working for the Lord is a way of finding freedom and fulfilment in work and involves an attitudinal change in our lives. Let's remember again that, if we spend more than half our waking hours working, and if that is done 'for the Lord', then we are well on the way to living the Christian life as it is meant to be.

Major challenges

In the day-to-day reality, the workplace confronts us with a wide range of other challenges to our Christian faith, challenges that need to be faced and overcome if the gap between our professed faith and our working life is to be closed. There are challenges to our integrity and honesty; there is the issue of how we treat people; the matter of our pride and ego and how we deal with success and failure; and the question of how much our sense of identity and worth is bound up in our work.

All these challenges provide us with opportunities to learn and grow, to trust God more, to develop Christian character, to stand up for what is right, to build relationships of mutual trust and respect, and, through it all, to reflect something of the character of Christ into the workplace. Let's consider these in turn.

Honesty and integrity

In any work situation we will face a number of tests to the honesty and integrity we profess. These tests can come in a number of forms. First, and most obviously, we can be tempted to steal from the petty cash, overclaim expenses and try to cheat on our tax return. We can also deceive our employers by not fulfilling our side of the work contract, by working fewer hours than we are paid for and deliberately working unproductively or taking sick leave when we are healthy.

We may also be tempted to abuse our position of trust to influence the appointment of friends or family into key positions, or to award contracts and purchases to our friends rather than to those who deserve them according to due process. As a young manager working for one public-sector organization, I found my recommendation to the board for award of a contract had been changed after I had submitted my report, but my signature had been left intact at the foot of the document. Several other similar abuses of privilege and process were subsequently discovered by the authorities. Both the chairman and the managing director of that organization were later convicted of fraud and imprisoned.

If you have the choice, it is best not to work for an organization which does not at least try to uphold basic principles of honesty and integrity.

Some Christians find those sorts of challenges to ethical honesty quite straightforward in theory. But in real life there are of course many shades of grey between the black-and-white extremes of clear wrong and right.

For example, you may never have stolen any money or defrauded anyone, but what about knowledge theft? A UK survey reported that 80% of professional people thought it likely that they would take some of their company's confidential information with them if they left to join another firm. If this is true, it is a worrying statistic for company owners and managers, and for society. Of course, the electronic age has made this sort of theft fairly simple, at least for the computer literate. Today a company's financial information, customer databases, technology and strategy can be quickly downloaded and carried away on a memory stick. Thirty years ago it would have been necessary to smuggle a whole truckload of paper reports out of the door to effect theft on the same scale!

Even if you walk out of the door without stealing information, you may be faced with how to use the confidential information that you carry in your head, particularly if you then join a competing firm, or if you are tempted to leak that information to the media. We all have to draw the line somewhere according to our conscience, enlightened by the Word of God.

The Bible calls us to work with honesty and integrity because we are working for the Lord.

The Old Testament book of Proverbs speaks very directly, as always, about honesty in business:

Food gained by fraud tastes sweet,
   but one ends up with a mouth full of gravel.
(Proverbs 20:17)

The LORD detests differing weights,
   and dishonest scales do not please him.
(Proverbs 20:23)

There is a very apt prayer for the Christian engaged in any sort of work, any day, in Psalm 25:

May integrity and uprightness protect me,
   because my hope, LORD, is in you.
(verse 21)

Perhaps the biggest mistake we can make is to confuse *what we do* and how we perform with *what we are*. It is all too obvious that the high-quality people we meet are not necessarily those who are at the top of the tree in politics, business, sport, entertainment or academia, but rather it is those who are honest, faithful and reliable in whatever position they are in. I am thinking here of a man I have worked with who is not afraid to take personal responsibility for whatever needs to be done, whether it's small things like turning off the lights and locking up, or major tasks like fixing the machinery safely; he is not afraid to speak up for what is right and, in terms of honesty, I would trust him with my life.

Such people are like gold, at work and in society, and should be treated with great respect, whatever their perceived position in the hierarchy.

Relationships

While high ethical standards of honesty and reliability in our dealings are fundamental to living as a Christian in the workplace, it is usually the way we treat other people, and our attitudes to them, that leaves the biggest impression. As has been said, with some over-generalization, there are two types of people: 'those who love things and use people' and 'those who love people and use things'. It is always very clear to others in the workplace (though not necessarily to ourselves) which category we are operating in at any given time. We can use others to advance our career, as a rung on the promotion ladder. Or we can value them.

Watch the social dynamics at play in a meeting or at a business dinner. There are those who automatically grab the best seat, the one near the boss, those who will talk only to those they consider worth talking to.

The great test, as always, is the golden rule. How do you feel when someone greets you while looking over your shoulder to see if there is someone more important they could be talking to? Then don't do it to others.

How do you feel when the person above you has no time to talk to you, and is not interested in your life? Then don't do it to them.

How would you feel if you heard someone say of you, 'She's a waste of space' or 'He's completely useless'? Then don't do it to others. We may not remember what people have said to us, or the circumstances in which they said it, but we usually remember how they made us feel at the time.

These contrasting attitudes have been characterized by non-Christian management consultants as the 'FIB' and 'ROC' culture respectively. 'FIB people' flatter the bosses, inflate their own contribution and blame others if things go wrong. 'ROC people' respect their bosses, take ownership of decisions, accept responsibilities and celebrate the success of others. If non-Christians can promote these standards for a harmonious and high-performance workplace, how much more should these attitudes characterize the Christian at work?

Relationships in the workplace will always be tested by *performance-related frustration*. Who has not returned from work at some time, seething with frustration about perceived non-performance of those above them, beneath them or alongside them? How do you react when people above you don't seem to care, when people below you don't perform to your expectation and support you, or when people alongside you don't cooperate or are simply 'bloody-minded'?

It happens, and we have to deal with it. How? By recovering a sense of proportion, by maintaining a sense of humour (an invaluable asset to defuse tension in any workplace) and, above all, by keeping a sense of our own shortcomings. Beware if you ever start to feel that 'everyone I work with is an idiot except me . . . !'

Pride and ego

Anyone who has spent time in the workplace will have experienced occasions when their pride has been hurt and their ego damaged. When promotions and special appointments are up for grabs and you miss out because someone else is preferred instead of you, how do you feel? More importantly, how do you deal with it; how do you react?

Or take a situation when someone else gets the credit for your ideas and hard work. I know a young schoolteacher who, together with an older colleague, was given the responsibility of putting on a special children's show for the parents. Nearly all the ideas and energy came from the younger teacher, but, at the end of the performance, when the head teacher was handing out the accolades, it was the older teacher who received all the credit.

This is a common problem in business, academia and scientific research, where stealing others' ideas can become a short cut to success.

How do you behave when you think you can do your boss's job much better than they can? Are you tempted quietly to undermine their authority at every opportunity, either by going over their head to their boss, or by criticizing them behind their back to whoever will listen? How do you deal with work situations in which the self-promoting, politically savvy people seem to advance up the greasy pole / corporate ladder, while many hard-working, equally competent people don't?

When our ego is damaged at work, there are four possible routes we can take. First, if we are fortunate enough to have the choice, we can simply resign: in the language of the children's playground, we can pick up our bat and ball and go home. Or second, we can enter a sort of adult sulk, described by a friend of mine as 'protracted temper at low key'. The result is usually a sort of stubborn non-cooperation, whereby we let it be known by our body language that we have been badly dealt with and we want everyone to know and take our side. Third, and most dangerously, we can plot our revenge. We may be tempted to work maliciously, to pay back those who have mistreated us. It's very sad to see people becoming bitter and twisted as they follow this route. As they try to make life miserable for the people they believe have wronged them, they often end up doing more emotional damage to themselves. The fourth route, the Christian way, is simply to see the situation as an opportunity to learn, to grow, to trust God to work things out, to submit to his authority and so to come through stronger.

A Christian friend, who held a management position in a large business, was one day informed by her boss that a new role was being established, with a new title. Another person had been recruited to lead the department and my friend was now to report to her. As my friend had spent years successfully building up her department and growing the business, her first reaction was one of anger, frustration and a sense of injustice. This was a major blow to her ego, as the new person would now receive all the credit for her ideas. My friend shared with me how she felt belittled in front of her colleagues when the new appointment was made public. Why had she been overlooked after performing so well? She then entered a second phase of reactions which involved letting others know how badly she had been treated. Openly she cooperated with her new boss, but she was no longer giving the job her best and no longer enjoyed her work. As she prayed over this, she had to confess her wrong attitude as a Christian and to learn again what it meant to do her work 'for the Lord', to give it her best and respect her new boss. As she did so, the whole atmosphere gradually changed, and my friend's reputation was actually enhanced, as others recognized how well she had handled herself, and the new situation which was not of her choosing. She came through this difficult period in her working life, and this testing experience for her Christian faith, both stronger and wiser.

It is almost inevitable that our work will provide many situations that will test us in terms of hurt to our pride and damage to our ego. They provide opportunities for us to live out our faith and apply what we say we believe about God, and to grow in character as we do so.

Identity and self-worth

To what extent are our self-esteem and our sense of identity based on our work and on the respect we earn through our work? If our sense of the value of our life is derived from what *we do*, rather than from what *we are*, then we have a problem, a problem that will be brought into sharp focus if ever we lose our job, or are demoted, or are forced to retire before we are ready.

At a recent work function, I met a former senior executive of a large company who had just retired. He introduced himself with the words: 'Hello, I'm Bill. I used to be somebody.' He was half-joking but, in the way he said it, he was unintentionally revealing his struggle with the loss of the position of power and respect he had once held. Clearly he felt the loss of a chunk of his own self-esteem and a part of his identity now that he was 'just a retiree', rather than the head of a large company.

Gareth Evans, a former Australian foreign minister, used the term 'relevance deprivation syndrome' to describe his experience after his political party had lost power in the national election. He faced a sudden change from playing on the international stage as a respected national leader before the election to being simply a member of the opposition afterwards.

It's hard when we move from a position in which we feel valued and respected, especially through redundancy, demotion or forced retirement, to one in which there is no-one seeking our instruction or direction, no-one concerned about what *we* think and no-one wanting our advice. It lays bare the whole question of our sense of self-worth.

In the movie *The Company Men*, Phil, one of three senior executives made redundant by a major corporation, makes this observation: 'You know the worst part . . . the world didn't stop; the newspaper still came every morning; the automatic sprinkler still shut off at six; Jeff next door still washes his car every Sunday . . . my life ended and nobody noticed.' This character was so overcome by his loss of self-respect and sense of worth that he took his own life. Out in the real world, forced redundancies can devastate lives and break up marriages.

The Christian gospel has wonderfully liberating good news at this point. The value of our life is measured not by what we own (our net worth in asset terms), nor by what we may or may not have achieved, but in the fact that God, who made us, has set the value of our life. He has shown us how much he thinks we are worth by giving his Son for us. God has set the same value on the poorest of the poor as on those we regard as the 'great and the good' of this earth. We are worth something because Christ paid the price of his own life for us.

If we carry this fundamental understanding of identity and worth into our daily work, we will have the right attitude. If you are in a position of authority at work, then it is only as a steward, and certainly only for a little while. If you have a job in which you feel you are doing something worthwhile, adding value and being valued for your contribution, then thank God. Many do not have the privilege of such an experience. Work can be an unhappy place when we feel our contribution is undervalued, but it's far worse when we feel unvalued for ourselves and who we are.

The way forward

If we want to live a whole life, a life of integrity, then we need to take to work every day the commitment to live a life that reflects the character of God (see chapter 3) and to build quality relationships of respect and care (chapter 4). As we do so, we will go to work with the right attitude. We will begin to see our work as part of our worship of God, and therefore whatever we do in word or deed, we will do it with sincerity and wholeheartedness, as for the Lord (Colossians 3:17, 23). Try this out in real situations:

> . . . when there seems no point in what you are doing
> . . . when others undervalue what you do
> . . . when others claim credit for your achievements
> . . . when others are playing power games to climb the tree
> . . . when you lose enthusiasm and energy for the task and it's hard for you to get out of bed in the morning

Try seeing work, not as a drudge or evil necessity, but as an opportunity to contribute to society through your gifts; an opportunity to live out your faith in difficult situations; to put into practice the godly qualities of honesty, integrity, justice, faithfulness, reliability and creativity; to learn and grow as a person, and to build quality relationships as you care for and encourage others. Aim to work in such a way that, when you are called to give an account to God for your life, you can look back with satisfaction, a sense of fulfilment and thankfulness to God for what he has enabled you to do and for the way he has helped you to do it.

Try working for the Lord and you will find your life changes. Work will become an act of service. Doing it whole-heartedly – without a divided heart – means that awful gap between the person you are in your 'Christian world', and who you are in the workplace, gradually closes.

Reflection

Read Colossians 3:17 and 3:23–24.

What does it mean in practical terms for you to do your work 'in the name of the Lord Jesus' and 'for the Lord'?

Read Romans 12:9–21.

What principles in this passage do you need to apply to your work situation?

What needs to change in your attitude to your work?

What do you need to do to improve relationships at your workplace?

How can your work become part of your worship of God?

6. A world of difference

Mind the gap
A warning to train passengers on the
London Underground and used in
metro systems worldwide

The gap between the world as it is and how it could be

In the 2006 film version of Zoë Heller's book, *Notes on a Scandal*, Sheba Hart, the schoolteacher played by Cate Blanchett, has this memorable line: 'My father always used to say, "Mind the gap". You know, the notice you see at railway stations warning about the gap between the train and the platform. Mind the gap "between life as you dream it and life as it is".'

The world is not as we would like it to be. The world is not as it could be, and it is certainly not as God designed it to be.

Helen Prejean, a Roman Catholic religious sister from New Orleans, spent years helping prisoners on death row. Her book, *Dead Man Walking*, describes her relationship with Elmo Patrick Sonnier, a prisoner consigned to death row in the Louisiana State Penitentiary. Sister Prejean has personally witnessed the execution of convicted criminals by electrocution. She once commented in an interview: 'It takes so long to form a human being, but only a few seconds to trash a human being.' It takes nine months being formed in the womb, years to grow to maturity, but one electric shock, one bullet, even one car crash, and life is over.

In all areas of life, we find that creativity takes time, effort and commitment, but destruction is the work of a moment. It is always easier to sink a ship than to raise one from the depths, easier to knock down than to build up.

This principle is true of relationships. Friendships, marriages or business partnerships, built up over years of love and trust, can be destroyed by a single act of deceit or betrayal. It is also true of careers. A great sportsman's reputation may be damaged by one act of drug taking, or a young person's future plans ruined in one drunken brawl, or a successful business or political career ended by one lapse into corruption or sexual misconduct.

A corrupted world

How do we make sense of a world in which destruction seems to be more powerful than creativity? Why is the world like that? The Bible tells us why in the first few pages. It opens with the statement that God is the Creator. This is the first and most basic truth revealed to us about God: 'In the beginning God created the heavens and the earth' (Genesis 1:1), and it was 'good'. He took delight in making beautiful things for us to enjoy (1 Timothy 6:17).

Genesis goes on to tell us that he made us, humankind, male and female, in his image. Therefore our creativity comes from him. The satisfaction and pleasure we get from creating something, and feeling good about it, come from God, as does the pleasure of making something for others to enjoy. This is part of the image of God that remains in every human being. That is why we derive such pleasure from creativity, whether decorating, building furniture, writing a book, developing a computer program or cooking a special meal. It is how we are wired.

The pain we feel when beautiful things, beautiful relationships and young lives are damaged also comes from our Creator. At the fall, God knew the experience of seeing the beautiful things he had made ruined by one act (Genesis 3).

The Genesis story brings us the first marital argument, the first play at the 'blame game' and the first futile attempts at self-justification. God made us in his image, but sin spoiled it. All of us are now imperfect. We are born with a virus that makes us tend to selfishness, jealousy, pride, fear, vanity, anxiety, envy, and so on. Every parent sees these traits appearing in their children from a very young age. All these failings spoil the image of God in us. Like a portrait that is scuffed and stained, but you can still see what the original was like, so our lives contain remnants of God's image and character.

Sin also spoils relationships. It separates us from God and from one another. Now we find it hard to get on with other people and living peacefully together. Perfect marriages, perfect families and friendships, perfect business relationships and perfect churches are not to be found on this earth. Sin has also damaged the created world, and the way we interact with it. As we continue to exploit and pollute our environment in an unsustainable way, each successive generation reaps the results of the abuse of its predecessor.

But sin does not just spoil; it destroys. When sin entered the world, death came with it: the next generation brought the first murder when Cain killed his brother Abel out of jealousy (Genesis 4). Sin leads to death, like an incurable cancer.

The Genesis story is widely ridiculed by non-believers. But here, in the first few pages of the Bible, we find the reasons why the world is as it is, why there is sickness, hatred, violence and killing, child abuse, marriage breakdown and war. The Bible tells us that this world is not as God made it.

A better world?

I listened recently to an interview with Sir Richard Attenborough, the movie actor and director, in which he made quite clear that he was *not* a religious man. However, he did have faith that 'one day good would triumph over evil in the world'. He was painfully aware of the gap between the world as it is and the world that he could envisage, one in which people would live in peace and where there would be no more war. We can all imagine a better world. Perhaps the ability to do that is also a part of the remnant of the image of God left in us.

The Old Testament prophet Isaiah was even more aware of this gap than most of us. He had been given a revelation by God of the new heaven and the new earth, which God would one day make when this damaged, dying world finally ends. He prophesied the coming of a 'new Jerusalem', which contrasted starkly with his experience of life in the city. In beautiful poetic language, Isaiah describes what life will be like when God lives among his people:

> They will beat their swords into ploughshares
>   and their spears into pruning hooks.
> Nation will not take up sword against nation,
>   nor will they train for war any more.
> (Isaiah 2:4)

Isaiah saw a world as it one day will be, a world in which people will live in harmony with one another and with God's creation (Isaiah 11:6–9).

But Isaiah also lived and worked in Jerusalem in the eighth century BC. It was a society in decline, with a failed leadership, violence and fear in the streets, and a religion that had lost its life, spiritual power and moral authority. Both the people and their leaders were complacent about the state of their society and were seemingly blind to what was coming. But Isaiah saw the root cause of the problem all too clearly:

> Woe to the sinful nation,
>> a people whose guilt is great,
> a brood of evildoers,
>> children given to corruption!
> They have forsaken the LORD;
>> they have spurned the Holy One of Israel
>> and turned their backs on him.
> (Isaiah 1:4)

A gap had opened up between the people and their God.

As a prophet of God, Isaiah had to live with the tension of these two contrasting pictures equally clear in his mind: life as one day God will make it, and the awful reality of the present.

This gap was a real problem for the early Christians living in the days of the Roman Empire, not just intellectually, but physically and practically. On the one hand, they saw and believed in Jesus' promise of heaven, glory, peace and joy. On the other hand, their experience was that of living with the threat of imprisonment, torture or death.

The world is not what we want it to be, nor even how we envision it could be. There is a gap between the better world we desire and our present experience; a gap between the future world that God has promised and life in this corrupted world now. But we have God's promise that he is working his purposes out, amid all the pain and violence, to close the gap forever. And nothing will prevent him.

But what is *our* responsibility in all this? Are we just to bewail all the evil we see or, worse, bury our head in the sand while we wait for God to act? No! We are called by God to make a difference for good *in this world* through acts and attitudes of creativity and renewal, to be part of the solution, not just part of the problem. The Bible gives us a number of different metaphors for the role God has for us. We are to be his *servants*, doing what he commands, being God's hands and feet on this earth. We are to be *witnesses* to Jesus, our Lord and Saviour, testifying to the truth revealed to us in Scripture and living a life consistent with our words (Acts 1:8; 1 Peter 3:15).We are to be like fruit-bearing trees that produce the fruit of godly character and bless the lives of others (John 15). All these are whole-of-life roles, which are to characterize all of our life, all of the time. But here let's reflect on two other roles God has for each of us: to be salt and light, also a 'whole-of-life' role; and the particular task of being a 'rebuilder' with God of what sin has broken down.

Salt and light – making a difference

Businesses and sports teams, working to develop and succeed, look to recruit 'impact players': people who will make a difference to the results, who will inspire those around them and lift their performance, and who will make an impact for good.

Christians are also called by God to be impact players, to make a difference to the society in which we live. As Jesus says, 'You are the salt of the earth . . . You are the light of the world . . . let your light shine before others, that they may see your good deeds and glorify your Father in heaven' (Matthew 5:13–16).

Salt prevents decay. When I lived in the East African bush, we used to salt the meat and hang it in strips to dry. Long before the days of refrigeration, salt was used as a preservative: it can be rubbed into meat to prevent natural decay. So every Christian is to have the effect of constraining and combating the decaying and destructive effects of evil in the world.

Light dispels darkness. So Jesus' followers are to dispel the darkness of evil and ignorance about God, through their words and through the quality of their lives. Think for a moment of a Christian you know whom you love and respect. Perhaps someone who shared the gospel with you and brought you to faith in Christ, or one who cooked meals and looked after your children when you were sick, or spent time with you after a bereavement. Maybe one who stood up for Christian principles in the face of scorn and opposition, or one whose faith and patience in the face of personal sorrow so impressed you. Then think how much poorer your life (and this world) would have been without them. Such people have been faithful to their calling. Thank God for their example. Now it is up to us. God calls you and me to be salt and light to others.

As we have seen, Christians are salt and light as they reflect God's character into the world, as they form faithful loving relationships, as they experience God's recreative power. In other words, simply by being truly Christian, we can have the effect, knowingly or unknowingly, of making a difference for good in the world.

But God calls us also to be *proactive* in this calling, to set out intentionally to live and work for the purpose of serving him and being a witness to his reality and power. He calls us to *spread* the gospel and to *live* the gospel. God equips us all with different gifts and personalities for this purpose, so that each of us can carry out the specific tasks God has set us on earth to do.

As we saw in the last chapter, we are all called to make a difference in some way through our daily work. God may also call us to make a difference through serving our community in politics, in voluntary work in hospitals or community groups, or in our churches. We may have a particular gift in visiting and caring for people, or in the raising and administering of money. We may be called to some great public task – founding a charitable organization, standing up for injustice, using our democratic right to demonstrate and lobby against a law or policy we believe to be wrong, welcoming refugees, helping the homeless, alcoholics or drug addicts.

When I think of those I have known who have made an impact for good, I think particularly of a friend who took the trouble to write me a thirty-six-page letter explaining the gospel when I first came to faith. I think of the man who regularly went out of his way to give lifts to those in his neighbourhood who needed transport and to visit those who were housebound through sickness or old age. I think of the woman who will always go the extra mile in terms of showing practical kindness to those she meets. I remember Dave, best man at my wedding, a wonderfully gifted teacher at a tough inner-city school, who died of colon cancer in his thirties and who led his wife to faith in Christ as he was dying.

I also think of those who have moved away from their homeland, such as my friend Paul from London. In 1974, after being rejected by a missionary organization, he made his own way to Mauritius to begin working to help some of society's rejects in the Indian Ocean islands. In the years that followed, he founded a succession of not-for-profit businesses which provided useful, creative employment to young people with various disabilities, and set up a learning centre for children with special needs which continues to this day.

All these people made a difference out of love for Christ. They were all 'salt and light' in different ways. Whether in low- or high-profile roles, whether in our local town or overseas, we are called to serve in one way or another. Just how we serve will depend on our age, our gifts, our training, the time we make available, and our mental and physical attributes, but in some way God calls us all to be actively involved in his work of impacting society for good. We need to consider what it is that he wants us to do.

Rebuilding and restoring

God is a builder. The writer to the Hebrews reminds us that Abraham 'was looking forward to the city with foundations, whose architect and builder is God' (11:10). And 'God is not ashamed to be called their God, for he has prepared a city for them' (11:16). He is creating and building a new city, a heavenly one. When this world finally ends, God will have something else ready.

The Lord Jesus Christ is a builder. He said, 'I will build my church, and the gates of Hades will not overcome it' (Matthew 16:18).

As we saw in chapter 3, God is the great Recreator and Restorer. He is also the great Rebuilder:

I will restore David's fallen shelter –
　I will repair its broken walls
　and restore its ruins –
　and will rebuild it as it used to be.
(Amos 9:11)

Through the prophet's words, God promises to rebuild his broken-down people, despite their past failure.

When the world invades our living room via the TV news, it is easy to feel overwhelmed by its decay and darkness. Breakdown in marriages, families, communities and nations is causing immense distress to millions of people – even as you read this. In the midst of all the forces that are breaking down our societies, God has a part for us to play in his work of building strong Christian lives, marriages, families and churches, and in rebuilding what is broken down.

Nehemiah – a leader who made a difference

Perhaps the best model in the Bible for this work of rebuilding is found in the story of Nehemiah, a man whose work was part of his worship, and in whom there was no discernible gap between the way he lived and worked and what he professed to believe.

He was called by God to the specific task of rebuilding the walls of Jerusalem, which had been broken down by the conquering Babylonian army many years before. Nehemiah experienced, and responded to, the call of God. He then faithfully fulfilled his calling in the face of great opposition, from both outside and inside the community that he was seeking to help. Nehemiah truly made a difference for good in his generation.

The book of Nehemiah opens in the year 445 BC. Nehemiah was a senior official in the court of Artaxerxes, the Persian king. One day he heard news that moved him to prayer and tears. He heard that the walls of Jerusalem, the great city of his beloved homeland, had been broken down and the gates had been 'burned with fire' (Nehemiah 1:3).

At this point we might ask ourselves, 'What will move *us* to pray and weep?' In the daily onslaught of news about terrorism, death, famine and injustice, what things move us?

Or are we so hardened by the twenty-four-hour news channels that the world's problems no longer affect us? After all, we have enough troubles of our own. Of course, we cannot carry the burden of the world's problems on our own shoulders; nor are we meant to. Just carrying one person's pain can nearly crush us, be it the sorrow of our best friend's marriage breakdown, the death of a child or disappointment over a friend's redundancy notice. But if we are to be close to the heart of God, we will feel something of his pain over the state of the world, something of how Jesus felt when he wept over Jerusalem.

The need and God's call

Nehemiah began to realize that God was calling him to do more than feel upset about this situation! Nehemiah saw the need and was moved to tears by it, but he also realized that he was in a position to *do something* about it, and he responded. As the book of Nehemiah tells us, he led the people in the rebuilding of the broken-down walls and, perhaps more importantly, he led the long process of rebuilding a broken-down people, restoring their sense of identity and purpose as the people of God.

This raises an important question. In all the needs of the world, how do I know what particular task God is calling *me* to do, or, as some put it, when does a 'need' become to me a 'call'? If we look at the book of Nehemiah, we find the answer to that question. A need becomes a call to us when it really starts to matter to us and when we realize that we are in a position, perhaps a unique position, to do something about it.

I learned this lesson as a new Christian in my twenties. I was sitting in the church we attended and noticed a number of children aged between eleven and fifteen looking totally bored, as children of that age often do in formal church services. Why doesn't somebody start a group for them in which they can *enjoy* learning about God? As that thought lodged in my mind, it began to dawn on me that I was in a position to start such a group. The question 'Why don't they . . . ?' changed to 'Why don't I . . . ?' That need became a call to me, because it started to matter to me that children would miss the opportunity to learn what it really meant to be a Christian, in a way they could relate to, and I also realized that I could change that. So we started a group, and it continued for many years.

Prayer, planning and preparation

The story of Nehemiah makes an inspiring read. He was a man who *prayed* for guidance, for practical help, for God to bring the king himself to help him and for victory over those who opposed his God-given mission. He was also a man who *planned*. He did not launch into this huge task without a lot of pre-planning about the materials he needed, how he would organize the workers and schedule their tasks. He was not too spiritual to see the value of good planning. Nor was he so confident in his management skills that he dispensed with the continual need to pray and seek guidance from God.

He was very thorough in his *preparation*. Before telling the people what he believed God intended him to do, he went out on his own at night and undertook a reconnaissance mission around the walls, so that he fully understood the size of the task he was taking on. We can learn a lot here. Maybe God wants you to start visiting a lonely person, to provide emotional and practical support to a lone parent or to take on a leadership role in a young people's group. You know that it will involve time, energy and stress. You also know that, once you start, you will find it hard to back out, and so you may be reluctant to commit. Nehemiah must have felt like that, as he toured the broken-down walls at night. Perhaps the thought, 'Why on earth did I take this on?', might have entered his mind.

Like Nehemiah, we are wise to prepare well, take time to pray through the situations to which we think God is calling us, and ask for his guidance and strength along the way.

Nehemiah was a great leader. He had the God-given ability to unite the people with a sense of vision and purpose, showing them what they could achieve if they worked together. It's always good in any role, in any form of Christian service, if you can gather others around you to help, to pray with you, to be there when you need advice. It is a lonely road to take on big challenges for God on your own.

Halfway weariness

It is one thing to have a vision and great ideas; it is quite another to put them into practice and finish the task. Nehemiah persisted until his job was done. He did not give up. This is a much-underrated quality.

When the wall was half-built, the people started to get discouraged at the size of the task they had taken on and their lack of strength. Their commitment started to waver. They were experiencing a typical 'halfway-weariness' syndrome.

Say you wake up one morning and resolve to redecorate your living room. You start with great energy and enthusiasm. You move the furniture out, cover the floor and wash down the walls. The day wears on and you start to feel tired. There is still so much to do and, with mess all around, you begin to wish you hadn't started. The people in Jerusalem felt like that. You may feel like that halfway through the year, as you begin to wonder if you did the right thing in taking on that teaching role at your local church, or that commitment to help a difficult person who seems so unappreciative of the time and energy you are giving.

How did Nehemiah deal with this sense of weariness in the people, and what can we learn from him? First and foremost, he inspired the people: 'Remember the Lord, who is great and awesome, and fight for your families, your sons and your daughters, your wives and your homes' (Nehemiah 4:14). When we grow weary and feel like giving up, we may need to turn our focus back on God and his mighty power and remember that, whenever we are doing his work, we will need to learn to fight spiritual battles (see Ephesians 6:10–18).

Overcoming opposition

Rebuilding can be slow work. Nehemiah's task of rebuilding the walls was finished in fifty-four days, but his bigger task of rebuilding the broken-down people of God went on for many years. The work of rebuilding the life of just one individual damaged by child abuse, of one person scarred by a marriage breakdown or impacted by a job failure, can take years. Any role we take on in Christ's name will inevitably involve major challenges and opposition, and will demand our persistence and commitment. Jesus warned us to expect it.

Nehemiah certainly faced great opposition. Again, we can learn a lot from how he handled these difficulties. He encountered opposition at the beginning of the project, during the project and after the project had been completed. As it became clear that the people were succeeding in their task of rebuilding, so opposition from outside God's people increased. First the enemies started mocking what he was doing; then they turned to anger and insult (4:1), and finally to organized, concerted opposition (4:7–8). Nehemiah calmly dealt with this by encouraging the people to *pray* and preparing them to *fight*.

Moreover, Nehemiah encountered opposition from *within* the people, and this is sometimes harder to deal with than opposition from outside. He also had to deal with grumbling and complaints about injustice. Anyone who has started any task involving leadership of a team of people will know how he felt at this point: 'Why am I always left to stay late and clear up the mess?' 'Why does she never volunteer for the dirty jobs?' In your service, you might have heard this sort of grumbling, and perhaps you have been guilty of it yourself. It is very destructive and diverts attention away from the main task.

The third way in which Nehemiah experienced opposition was in the form of personal attacks. The earlier attacks were against the people and the project, but later it became personal. First, his enemies tried to entice him away from his work, and then they attacked his motives and integrity. Finally, they issued a death threat. Nehemiah realized that this attempt at intimidation was aimed to stop the rebuilding work, so he turned again to prayer and simply carried on with the job.

W. P. Nicholson, the late Irish evangelist, once famously commented, 'If the devil can't keep you from being *converted* he will bend all his power to get you *diverted*.' This was true for Nehemiah and it is true for all of us. Whenever we take on a God-given task to make a difference, we can expect opposition and pressure from all directions to divert us from what God has called us to do.

Nehemiah was a leader, but he had a servant heart. Like Jesus, he exercised his leadership by setting an example and serving the good of others. He was both a builder and a fighter. He longed to see the broken-down walls and the broken-down people rebuilt. He devoted himself to it and fought off all the opposition that came. He was also both a pray-er and a do-er. He was a spiritual man who loved God and brought all of life's issues to his God in prayer, but he was also a man of action who got things done.

He lived an undivided life. He was a man in whom there was no visible gap between what he professed to believe and how he lived, between his spiritual life and his daily work, between his faith and his passion for justice. But we learn more from Nehemiah than a good example to follow. We discover that God's work, done in God's way and in his time, will be fruitful: this is great encouragement for whatever task God has called us to do.

Nehemiah was called to a massive public task, and we may judge the work to which we have been called to be quite small and insignificant by comparison. But God may see it differently. Jesus promised a reward just for giving a cup of cold water to a thirsty child (Matthew 10:42). Who knows what seemingly small act of love and service done in Christ's name may be of greater value in eternity than all our most treasured achievements?

Whatever task we are called to, if we follow the same principles as Nehemiah did, then we will make a difference. We will impact on society for good, and we will be salt and light in the world.

Reflection

In what ways is God calling you to 'make a difference'?

What can you learn from the example of Nehemiah?

What practical steps do you need to take?

7. Wisdom at work

Teach us to number our days,
that we may gain a heart of wisdom.
(Psalm 90:12)

The gap between human wisdom and God's wisdom

When you come to know God, to respond to what Christ has done, there is a radical change in what you consider wise and foolish. Before, talk of God, of Christ and salvation seemed foolish. Reading the Bible seemed like a waste of time. Now, knowing God through Jesus Christ is what matters most to you. Now, the world of materialism, without answers to death, a world in which politics never seems to solve problems in any lasting way, a world of celebrity adulation and constant power struggles in which people strut around demanding respect they do not deserve – that is now foolishness.

God's wisdom is often contradictory to human wisdom:

'For my thoughts are not your thoughts,
   neither are your ways my ways,'
                     declares the LORD.
(Isaiah 55:8)

In the New Testament, the apostle Paul, a highly educated and intelligent man, asked rhetorically,

> Where is the wise person? Where is the teacher of the law? Where is the philosopher of this age? Has not God made foolish the wisdom of the world? For since in the wisdom of God the world through its wisdom did not know him, God was pleased through the foolishness of what was preached to save those who believe.
> (1 Corinthians 1:20–21)

Paul had come to understand the difference between human wisdom and God's wisdom. He goes on:

> Jews demand signs and Greeks look for wisdom, but we preach Christ crucified: a stumbling-block to Jews and foolishness to Gentiles, but to those whom God has called, both Jews and Greeks, Christ the power of God and the wisdom of God. For the foolishness of God is wiser than human wisdom, and the weakness of God is stronger than human strength.
> (1 Corinthians 1:22–25)

Where does wisdom fit into the theme of this book? How does it close the gaps? Wisdom is the gift God gives to help us live a life that is Christ-like in building others up, a life in which what we think and say is consistent with what we do: an undivided life. We need wisdom because we spend most of our waking hours, not in church or at prayer, but in the hurly-burly of life. We have to speak, act and react in seemingly mundane situations: in the shops, at work and at home. Most of us don't face major crisis decisions every day. We do, though, make hundreds of small decisions every day, which affect others and may influence the direction of our lives. We have the Holy Spirit as our guide and the Bible as our teacher, but these point us to wisdom as a precious gift that we should prize very highly.

The value of wisdom

What is worth giving up everything to gain? What is more valuable than precious jewels, and absolutely essential for us in order to steer our way through all the challenges, difficulties and temptations of life? What is it that, when applied in the home, the workplace and the routine of everyday life, closes the gap between what we profess to believe and how we actually live? The Bible's answer is 'wisdom'.

Yet wisdom is a greatly undervalued quality in our society. It is not on most people's wish-list.

Recently I watched some film clips of young people being interviewed about what they wanted from life. The answers were predictable: happiness, money, success, a good job, a happy marriage and children, a good home, travel to exciting places, and so on. Wisdom did not figure in any of the answers. As we grow older, our priorities change. We want good health, sufficient money to live on in retirement, and security, but it is still doubtful if wisdom is high on anyone's list of 'must-haves'.

It was said of Jesus that, as a child, he 'grew and became strong; he was filled with wisdom' (Luke 2:40). Most societies today place great emphasis on growing physically: on healthy diets, exercise and avoiding obesity. We may put an even stronger emphasis on education, on learning, on preparation for a career and a useful role in society. But we hear very little about growth in wisdom. We give great respect to the rich, the attractive, the celebrities, the clever and the athletic. But not to the wise.

To understand what the Bible means by wisdom, and why it is so valuable, we need to turn to the book of Proverbs. There we find that 'wisdom' includes understanding, discipline, prudence, knowledge and discretion. You might say that it is really just 'common sense' but, in truth, wisdom is very un-common: 'She [wisdom] is more precious than rubies' (Proverbs 3:15). Men and women can succeed in life, rise to the top of their profession, and still not have true wisdom, because 'The fear of the LORD is the beginning of wisdom' (9:10). Without knowing God, you cannot discover the meaning or purpose of your life, and therefore you cannot be truly wise. Wisdom is not to be confused with our IQ level, with learning, shrewdness or intellectual ability, with being street-smart or business-savvy. It starts with recognizing that there is a God who made you, and to whom you are accountable.

Recognizing wisdom

How then do we recognize wisdom? We see it in people's attitudes, in their understanding, in their words and actions. The wise person has the right *attitude* to life. He recognizes how short life is and sets priorities in the light of that. Psalm 90 contains this prayer:

> Teach us to number our days,
>   that we may gain a heart of wisdom.
> (verse 12)

The fool does not think about death. He does not want to face up to life's big questions: 'What happens when I die?' or 'What is my life for?' The wise person recognizes that we will die – that the sands of time are always running out. Therefore he wants to spend his life getting to know God and doing the will of God. If we are wise, we will ask God to help us not to waste the precious days he has given us, but rather to use them wisely and do what is truly worthwhile.

Wisdom involves *wise thinking*. A wise person has under-standing of the ways of God and the hearts of people. Jesus 'knew what was in each person' (John 2:25). He could see what motivated people and he frequently exposed it, to the discomfort of his hearers. Wisdom here is the ability to weigh up what to do and say in difficult situations and to discern the true motives of others. According to Proverbs 2:11,

> Discretion will protect you,
>   and understanding will guard you.

King Solomon prayed, while still a young man, 'Give your servant a discerning heart to govern your people and to dis-tinguish between right and wrong' (1 Kings 3:9). This is the sort of wisdom needed by parents and by anyone involved in leadership or counselling. Wisdom, though, is not just about thinking wise thoughts. It is the application of those thoughts to life, exercising 'emotional intelligence' in practical situations.

True wisdom is seen in *speaking wisely*. The wise person knows when to speak and when to keep silent. Going into a work meeting, a colleague advised me (tongue-in-cheek), 'Far better to keep silent and be thought a fool than to open your mouth and remove all doubt!' I have learned that not everyone who asks me a question wants to hear my answer! I may need to keep my mouth shut and listen further in order to understand what lies behind the question before I launch into giving my opinions. When people are faced with bereavement or sickness, and are asking, 'Why?', the wisest response is sometimes simply to listen and show that you care: 'The hearts of the wise make their mouths prudent' (Proverbs 16:23).

The wise person knows what to say when he does open his mouth:

> Gold there is, and rubies in abundance,
>> but lips that speak knowledge are a rare jewel.
>
> (Proverbs 20:15)

The wise person knows *the right time to say the right thing*. In dealing with other people, there is a time to teach and rebuke and a time to offer a quiet word of encouragement. One of the most beautiful proverbs highlights this issue:

> Like apples of gold in settings of silver
>> is a ruling rightly given.
>
> (Proverbs 25:11)

To say the right thing, at the right time, to the right person, is to bring some beauty and value into the world.

Unwise words can be very damaging. Some years ago I attended an international business conference in Hong Kong. There were about 500 delegates, plus their wives and partners, from around the world. The after-dinner speech was given by the global chair of the organization sponsoring the conference. He opened with a long and very crude joke, which was received by the audience with stony silence. In just five minutes, he had destroyed his image as a man of integrity and wisdom, in front of a large international gathering.

Most of us know what it is like to blurt something out, only to regret it later. Words come out of the mouth like toothpaste from a tube, and you can never put them back in.

True wisdom is seen not just in wise thinking and wise words, but also in *wise actions*. Proverbs has a lot to say about fair dealing in business, kindness to the poor, avoiding sexual temptation, the virtue of hard work – about practical godly living and prudence:

> All who are prudent act with knowledge,
>   but fools expose their folly.
> (Proverbs 13:16)

Prudence is not just doing the right thing; it is doing the right thing *at the right time*.

The story of Abigail, who was married to Nabal and later became King David's wife, is a great example of wisdom in action in a very tense situation. Nabal had foolishly wronged David, who had then sworn to take his revenge. Abigail saw the dangerous situation developing and acted swiftly, decisively and with great wisdom. She sent out delegations with gifts to meet David and followed this up herself by asking for David's forgiveness for her husband's stupidity.

David listened to her plea and halted his vengeful mission. He said to Abigail, 'Praise be to the LORD, the God of Israel, who has sent you today to meet me. May you be blessed for your good judgment and for keeping me from bloodshed this day and from avenging myself with my own hands' (1 Samuel 25:32–33). Notice how Abigail's wise thinking and wise actions not only saved the lives of innocent people; they also saved David from having murder on his conscience for the rest of his life. We would do well to pray for wisdom for our leaders whose decisions affect the lives of others.

If the author of the book of Proverbs were writing today, I suspect he would have something to say about wisdom in this age of instant electronic communication. We now take it for granted that, at the press of a button, we can communicate instantaneously to a massive audience globally, via Twitter, blogs, YouTube and, of course, by email.

I have learned the hard way about the damage that can be done by instant messages and emails sent without reflecting wisely first. For the first time in human history, a personal message sent from one person to another can be forwarded to millions in a moment. It's even worse if we type in the wrong addressee and send off an email containing critical or confidential comments.

Perhaps you know what it is like to search hastily for the recall key, only to find your message has already been read, and then to reach for the phone to make your apologies! Similarly, any photo, video clip or message posted on our website, blog or Facebook page can be quickly seen by millions. We need to be wise in the confidential information we share on social network sites. Unwise 'tweeting' is drawing increasing numbers into libel actions. Parents need to be wise about which photos of their young children they choose to make public. Indeed, we all need wisdom at times just to slow down in the pressure of daily life. It is wise to reflect on what we have written and how it will be interpreted, *before* we press the send button.

The wisdom of Jesus

If we want an example of wisdom, we need only look at Jesus Christ. He knew when to keep silent, when there was nothing more to be said, for example when he stood before Pilate, the Roman governor who condemned him to death. Whenever Jesus did speak, all his words were full of truth. They showed deep understanding of the people he was speaking to. He always spoke the right words at the right moment.

One situation perfectly illustrates Jesus' wisdom in action. The Pharisees and teachers of the law brought to him a woman who had been caught in the act of adultery, which, according to the strict letter of the law, deserved death by stoning, as in some Islamic societies today. They asked Jesus what should be done with her, trying to trap him.

Jesus said nothing, but just bent down and started writing in the sand with his finger. After a while, he straightened up and said these famous words: 'Let any one of you who is without sin be the first to throw a stone at her.' The people started to drift away. John notes that the older ones left first. Perhaps they were more aware of their own failings than the young were. When there was no-one left, Jesus asked the woman, 'Has no one condemned you?' 'No one, sir,' she replied. Jesus then added, with great wisdom, 'Then neither do I condemn you . . . Go now and leave your life of sin' (see John 8:1–11). In this incident, Jesus showed wisdom in keeping silent and avoiding futile debate, wisdom in his penetrating words to the accusers, and wisdom in his words of forgiveness and guidance to the woman.

In a second, equally well-known incident in which we see Jesus' wisdom in action, some Pharisees again came to him with a trick question: 'Is it right to pay the poll-tax to Caesar or not?' (Matthew 22:17). This was a clever attempt to lure Jesus into a trap. They must have spent some time coming up with this gem. If he said no, then they could go to the Roman authorities and have him charged with inciting rebellion. If he said yes, he would lose the support of the common people, who hated the Roman oppression. Jesus invited them to show him a coin and asked whose image was on it. The emperor's head was on the coin. Then came Jesus' words of wisdom: 'Give back to Caesar what is Caesar's, and to God what is God's.' Matthew adds the comment: 'When they heard this, they were amazed [at his wisdom]. So they left him and went away' (22:15–22).

Wisdom – a gift of God

How then do we get wisdom? The Bible's answer is simple. It is a gift from God: 'If any of you lacks wisdom, you should ask God, who gives generously to all without finding fault, and it will be given to you' (James 1:5). Our prayers reveal what is truly important to us. Just reflect for a moment on what you pray for most often and with the most sincerity. Maybe you pray for a job, for a life partner, for success at work, for a sick friend or relative, for your children, for guidance in the difficult decisions you face. If the statistics of your prayer life were analysed, I wonder what the most prayed-for items would be.

Here is a call to put prayer for wisdom high on our list. We all make mistakes and we need wisdom to navigate through the complexities of life and, by our words and actions, to help others do the same. Remember the story of King Solomon. When he was still young, God invited him to ask whatever he wanted and it would be given. Solomon asked for wisdom to govern and lead the people. God was pleased with this request and he promised Solomon that, because he had his priorities right and had asked for wisdom rather than riches, he would also be given long life and success (1 Kings 3:1–15). That may – or may not – happen for us, but the lesson of the book of Proverbs is that wisdom *by itself* is to be valued very highly. It should be high on our wish-list.

The wisdom of Proverbs

In order to get wisdom, then, we need to ask God to give it to us. We need to learn from Jesus, the ultimate human example of wisdom in action. We also need to study and apply the book of Proverbs. If you are not yet familiar with the book, then start reading! It's a treasure chest of rich things and it repays study. It paints some timeless, graphic word pictures to help us understand what foolishness and wisdom look like in the real world.

For example, there is the married man, tempted to break his marriage vows by the attractive young woman whose lips 'drip honey'. But then comes the warning that, if you fall for the temptation, it will surely end in tears and bitterness (5:4). Playing with sexual sin in any form is like 'scooping fire into your lap' (see 6:27), and you are likely to get burned.

There is the challenge to the lazy one:

How long will you lie there, you sluggard? . . .
A little sleep, a little slumber,
   a little folding of the hands to rest.
(6:9–10)

We might picture someone sprawled out on the couch, wasting hours flicking through the cable network channels, or surfing the net, or tweeting everyone about anything, but helping no-one and producing nothing.

Or what about the conman, the thief 'who winks maliciously with his eye . . . motions with his fingers, who plots evil with deceit in his heart' (Proverbs 6:13–14)? Here is a picture of someone offering to show you how to 'make a bit on the side', to take some short cuts and cheat someone or avoid paying what is legally due: an entrance fee, a tax charge, or simply lifting something from the local store because no-one is watching. Proverbs readily acknowledges that such offers may look very attractive at first:

Stolen water is sweet;
>   food eaten in secret is delicious!
> (9:17)

But for all those entering this particular 'house of folly', it will inevitably end badly:

Little do they know that the dead are there,
>   that her guests are deep in the realm of the dead.
> (9:18)

The 'bottom line' of the whole book is simply this: Don't mess your life up with stupid acts; don't fall for the seeming attractiveness of unfaithfulness, laziness and dishonesty. Rather, listen to the words of the wise (1:5), listen to your parents (1:8) and learn to reverence God (1:7). Then discretion will protect you, and understanding will guard you (2:11). It is only fools who despise wisdom and instruction (1:7).

But the book of Proverbs contains much more than warnings. It also presents the beautifully positive picture of the undivided life: the godly woman (chapter 31), who runs her home and her business with dignity, respect and generosity; and the godly man, who cares for the poor, faces the future with confidence and sleeps peacefully at night with a clear conscience (3:23–27). The lives of such people are characterized by love and faithfulness, qualities at the core of their being which also beautify their lives:

Let love and faithfulness never leave you;
>   bind them round your neck,
>   write them on the tablet of your heart.
> (3:3)

As we live out our faith in this complex world, which confronts us with so many hard choices, we are wise if we allow the book of Proverbs, and indeed the whole of Scripture, to guide and teach us.

Reflection

Think of someone you know whom you regard as wise.

How has their wisdom shown itself to you and to others, in their words or actions?

Ask God for the gift of wisdom.

8. Enjoying success

Success is a lousy teacher.
It seduces smart people into thinking they can't lose.
Bill Gates

The gaps created by success

Success brings out both the best and the worst in us.

It brings out the best because to succeed at anything usually involves hard work, commitment and sacrifice: qualities worthy of respect in any society. But it also brings out the worst.

Our own success quickly turns to pride, even to arrogance and selective memory, when we underplay, intentionally or otherwise, the part played by others in that success. Our success can widen the distance between us and others, who may put us on a pedestal and credit us with wisdom and virtues we do not possess. We see this frequently when football players, rock stars and other 'celebrities' struggle to keep their feet on the ground in the face of the adulation and financial rewards heaped upon them.

Before I get too critical of such people, I find myself asking how well I would have managed at the age of twenty, at the centre of attention and being paid huge amounts of money. How well would I have coped with the adulation of the fans?

How would I have responded to media pressure and the temptation to pontificate on political and social issues of which I had very little knowledge? Not well, I suspect!

On the other side of the coin, when others succeed where we have failed, envy usually rears its ugly head. Be honest: how do you feel when your friend is dating the person you want for yourself? When someone gets the job or promotion you thought you deserved? The way we handle our own success, and the way we deal with the success of others, tells us a lot about our character. It quickly reveals our true values and the extent of our own sinfulness. Pride and self-centredness about our own success, or envy at the success of others, also put a great strain on our relationships. Moreover, these particular manifestations of sin distance us from God.

What is success?

If I had sent you a greeting at the beginning of the year, wishing you 'every success in the year ahead', what would have come into your mind? How would you measure success in your life? What do you want to achieve in your relationships, in your work, in your personal life?

Maybe you are one of those very focused and organized people who has written down your goals for this year, and now you're going all out to achieve them.

Even if (like me) you haven't written them down, you probably have a pretty clear idea in your mind as to what will constitute 'success' for you.

Or you might be an avid reader of those self-help books that promise to reveal the secrets of success in business and in your personal life.

When John Paul Getty, who used to be America's richest man, was asked the secret of his success, he reportedly replied,

'Rise early, work hard . . . strike oil.' The first two sound like good advice, and all I can say about the third is: 'Good luck!' That sort of success can be an elusive goal!

When we speak of 'success', we usually mean the achievement of a goal. We succeed by winning the match, getting the job or passing the exam. We succeed when we finish the task, when we renovate the house, finish the marathon or complete our studies, or when we receive the promotion, reward or recognition we have sought. Success seems to be about getting, winning, completing or achieving.

But success is not just about the end result; it's also about the means to that end. It's not just about 'what'; it's also about 'how'. The business person can bribe their way to 'success'; the athlete can use drugs to gain victory, but in each case the quality of their achievement is massively diminished. Success is *not* just about getting and winning; it's also about becoming the people we want to be.

It is a relative measure. If you are one of the world's élite athletes, then fourth place in the Olympic final, just missing out on a medal, may look like failure. For most people, to compete in the finals, or to reach the Olympics at all, would be an outstanding success. Success has to be considered in the context of natural ability, opportunity and circumstance.

Furthermore, success is normally measured in relation to one particular area of life. Those successful in some areas may fall short in others. Brilliantly gifted artists and musicians may have disastrous personal relationships or poor business acumen. Great business people and movie stars may be failures in their marriages and as parents, despite outstanding success in their profession. Very few are able to cover all the bases.

It is also common for people to achieve success in one area of life at the expense of another. Others find themselves chasing success in one area of life which, unintentionally but inevitably, starts to damage their quality of life in another, and spoils their relationship with God in the process. The choices involved in establishing priorities are often painful and usually create tension.

I know a young sales manager of a large manufacturing company who was warned in his annual performance review that he had to put in more hours to progress his career. As he was already working a ten-hour day, this was not a reasonable demand. He was faced with the choice between his career and his wife and family – where should he invest those precious extra hours?

I also think of a young mother who is rapidly climbing up the corporate ladder. Her role requires frequent travel away from home for several days at a time. The strain on her marriage and home life is considerable.

Then there is the young couple who have taken on a massive mortgage to buy and renovate their dream home. Both are holding down full-time jobs and working on the house at weekends. Gradually, any time for worship and fellowship at their local church has been squeezed out, 'just while they fix the house up'. The costs of the rebuilding work are exceeding their budget (as building costs usually do!), and they are both lying awake at night wondering how they will cope. The stress is adversely affecting their relationship and their health. They feel locked on to a treadmill from which they can't escape, and their dream home is turning into a nightmare.

As I write, all three situations are unresolved. The people concerned are struggling to make hard decisions and to reset their priorities.

We may be faced with similar choices about what is most important to us: our marriage or our job, our integrity or our business success, a bigger house or greater enjoyment of our relationship with God? Naturally, most of us want the best of all worlds, but it simply isn't possible. Jesus warned us about this quite clearly: we cannot serve two masters; we cannot serve both God and Money (Matthew 6:24).

Sometimes we have to learn the hard way that we can't 'have it all'.

How does the Bible view success?

The Bible looks at success in a much wider and fuller way than simply acquiring material rewards and achieving recognition. Certainly, it sees success in terms of completing and fulfilling a task against all opposition, but the focus is on faithfulness and obedience, not on winning and acquiring. Jesus said that faithfulness in the little tasks entrusted to us will be rewarded by responsibility to undertake bigger tasks (Matthew 25:23). Faithfulness and obedience are what God values and rewards, not success itself. For example, in the parable of the talents (Matthew 25), those who added to their talents were successful because they had created wealth, but it was their *faithfulness* that was commended by God, not how much they had made through wise investment of what their master had given them.

The word 'success' appears only rarely in our English translations of the Bible. For example, there are the references in the Old Testament to Joshua, Hezekiah and Jehoshaphat. Joshua was promised success in his God-given task of leading the people into the Promised Land if he continued to obey the law of God (Joshua 1:7). King Hezekiah was successful in all he undertook because the Lord was with him (2 Kings 18:5–7). Jehoshaphat promised his people success in battle if they trusted in the Lord (2 Chronicles 20:20). So in these three situations, success was about military victory or about entering into the experience of what God had promised his people. Success came as God's people trusted and obeyed, and thereby enjoyed his presence with them. Their goal was to honour God by obeying his commands. Success was the by-product, not the goal.

But to understand the Bible's view of success, we need to take a broader view. Success, as we commonly understand it, is a very human-centred concept. We tend to see it as the result of *our* effort, *our* abilities and *our* commitment. The Bible takes a God-centred view. That is why it is described in other ways, such as prosperity, blessing and fruitfulness, to help us understand.

Prosperity

The words 'success' and 'prosperity' are often used interchangeably. But prosperity in the Bible is not just a matter of acquiring wealth and achieving personal goals. It has a strong ethical, spiritual and relational context. The *International Standard Bible Encyclopedia* summarizes the original meaning like this:

> Prosperity in the Old Testament connotes the realisation of goals (Gen 24:21, 40, 42, 56), success in labour (Gen 39:3, 23; 2 Chron 32:30), living in peace and safety (Deut 23:6; 1 Chron 14:7) . . . happiness (Lamentations 3:17), enjoying the benefits of familial relationships (Ruth 4:11) as well as acquiring and possessing material goods (Deut 28:11; 1 Kings 10:7; 1 Chron 29:23).[1]

Prosperity is linked to commitment and obedience to God's covenant, and comes with obligations, namely to share the blessings of prosperity in a fruitful way. It also comes with a warning. Those who do not acknowledge God in their prosperity (Jeremiah 10:21), and refuse to share their success with the poor, forfeit the blessings of the covenant (Deuteronomy 28:11; 29:9; 30:9).

Let's earth this biblical teaching in the here and now. If, for example, we are praying for our work to prosper, we are asking God for much more than just his help to make more money. We are asking for harmonious relationships in the workplace, for the trust and respect of our customers and for the ability to sleep peacefully at night because we are dealing with integrity and trusting God for the outcomes. We are asking God to bless the workplace and those we work with, in the fullest sense, to make them fruitful and to give them a sense of fulfilment. This is the biblical view of success. It needs to inform our praying and guide our behaviour.

Blessing

Psalm 84, for example, tells what it means to be blessed by God. The blessed ones are those whose lives are focused on the praise and worship of God (verse 4). They find their strength in their relationship with God, in running the race set before them, in living as pilgrims on this earth (verse 5). They go 'from strength to strength' (verse 7) throughout their lives, a vivid picture of God-given success. They trust in God in every aspect of life.

Furthermore, the psalmist makes clear his priorities, when he contrasts worldly success, wrongfully gained, with the experience of living in the blessing of God:

> I would rather be a doorkeeper in the house of my God
>> than dwell in the tents of the wicked.
> (84:10)

He recognizes that 'the LORD bestows favour and honour . . . ' (verse 11). Here is someone who sees clearly what is worthwhile and of lasting value, who looks to God to give 'success', rather than relying only on human effort.

Similarly, Psalm 1 paints a beautiful picture of the life of one who is blessed by God, the person who

> . . . does not walk in step with the wicked
> or stand in the way that sinners take
>   or sit in the company of mockers.
> (verse 1)

That person is like a tree planted by the water. The leaves provide shade; the roots go deep, and whatever they do prospers.

To enjoy the blessing of God is to be at peace with God, to have the face of God shine upon us, to know the keeping and saving grace of God (Numbers 6:22–26). In this frantic, pressured and sometimes frightening world, this is a priceless blessing.

Fruitfulness

Another biblical way of describing 'success' in the eyes of God is *fruitfulness*. God intends us to be fruitful. He intends us to produce in our lives the qualities of love, joy, peace, patience, kindness, goodness, faithfulness, gentleness and self-control (Galatians 5:22–23). To be fruitful means that our lives and our work enrich the lives of other people.

In Old Testament days, God looked in vain for this sort of fruitfulness from his people (Isaiah 5:1–2). Jesus looked for the same fruit from God's people during his three years of ministry on this earth, but he found none (Mark 11:12–13). He made clear that his purpose for his followers was to produce fruit that would grow only through a relationship of faith in him: fruit that would last (John 15:16).

God rates fruitfulness more highly than the material trappings of success. Amos, the Old Testament prophet, was called to deliver God's message to a society where the tangible rewards of success were being enjoyed – wealth, large houses, beautiful clothes and plenty of food and wine, at least for the privileged few – but there was no fruit, no justice, no godliness and no concern for the poor (see, for example, Amos 5 – 6).

Success then, in the biblical sense, is knowing God's blessing and sharing that with others with a generous spirit. It is enjoying a sense of freedom and fulfilment, and peace with God. To succeed is to live faithfully to God's call and to be fruitful. It is manifestly an experience to be celebrated, and for which we are to return thanks and worship to God when it is our privilege to enjoy it.

In whatever areas of our lives we want to be successful, let's make sure this deep biblical understanding of fruitfulness, prosperity and blessing moulds our thinking. Let's also remember that God may take us through some dark and testing times in the process.

Role models for success

What role models do you have for your view of 'success'? I have been inspired at various times by great adventurers, strong leaders, brilliant writers, speakers and inventors, and even by politicians! I am also thankful for all those I know who have lived fruitful, faithful, godly lives which have clearly been blessed by God. Their 'successes' will not even make the local paper, but, in terms of blessing other people, faithfulness to God's call and perseverance in the face of hardship, they tick all the boxes.

The Bible gives us a range of role models. The letter to the Hebrews contains 'a hall of fame' of God's great servants over the centuries (Hebrews 11). The list contains, as we might expect, the names of some men and women of faith who have *accomplished* great things for God: great leaders, heroic figures like David, Daniel and Abraham. But the list then goes on to include all those, named and unnamed, who have *suffered* great things for God. Note that God bestows on *them* the highest possible accolade: 'The world was not worthy of them' (Hebrews 11:38).

Jesus Christ is the perfect role model. He achieved great things: no single life has ever had such a huge impact on human history, but he also experienced tremendous suffering. When Jesus died, it appeared to be the ultimate failure. Here was a brilliant young teacher, a good and gifted man, cut off in the prime of life. Here was a man being publicly humiliated and cruelly treated, a figure of scorn and disgrace, being subjected to terrible pain. Death on a cross was, in that society, the ultimate failure.

And yet in God's plan, this was the ultimate success. How? Jesus was successful because he completed the work his Father had given him to do (John 17:4); he had run the race set before him right to the end (Hebrews 12:2); he was obedient in doing the will of his Father, even to the point of death (Philippians 2:8). He was successful because of what he achieved by all this: the salvation of a lost world. He was successful because he kept his eyes on 'the joy that was set before him' (Hebrews 12:2), which enabled him to endure to the end.

If your role models for success are all high-profile, wealthy individuals, then you need to turn to the Bible and think again. Look around you, starting with your local community, to all the unsung people who have maintained integrity, persisted in the battle for justice in society, shown the compassion of God in practical ways and been faithful to their marriage vows and other relationship commitments. Such people are the successful ones in the eyes of God. We need to learn from them.

Striving for success

If God rates people who have suffered great things for his sake
so highly, then we need to be wary of equating material success
with God's blessing. This, at least at first sight, is an attractive
and enticing doctrine. It provides a ready-made, seemingly
God-endorsed justification for indulging our love of power and
wealth. Beware of constructing a theology that assumes, 'I am
successful; therefore God must be pleased with me.' Let's
remember Jesus' warning to the rich fool, a successful businessman with his financial plan for retirement well prepared, but
who had got it all sadly wrong (Luke 12:13–21).

Conversely, let's not assume, 'I am not successful; therefore
God is not pleased with me.' It ain't necessarily so. What of
the millions of poor (both Christians and non-Christians)
around the world who seem unsuccessful in human terms?
Are they not loved by God?

As we have seen, there are Scripture passages (mainly in
the Old Testament) where God gives material blessings to the
obedient. But the references above show that some of the best
of God's people seem to be unsuccessful by material standards.
Let's be realistic: the apostle Paul pursued his trade as a
tentmaker, often working late into the night to support his
ministry. He didn't make a lot of money or win any awards
for doing that! Later he was a prisoner for many years and was
eventually executed. Our Lord Jesus Christ died a criminal's
death. God's call to us is not to pursue worldly success. It is
to 'seek first his [God's] kingdom and his righteousness'
(Matthew 6:33). If God does grant you wealth and power, use
them wisely, because, 'From everyone who has been given
much, much will be demanded' (Luke 12:48).

Material success in itself is not a worthy goal for the
Christian. Rather, we are to ' . . . make it our goal to please

him' (2 Corinthians 5:9). We will succeed in so far as we are faithful to our calling, and material success, if God grants it to us, is a by-product.

A changed view of success

Paul's view of success changed dramatically after his conversion. He tells us how in his letter to the Philippians.

In his pre-Christian days, Saul was a success, on several counts. He came from an élite tribe (Benjamin); he belonged to the right political party (the Pharisees); he was highly educated and had studied under a prestigious teacher (Gamaliel); and he came from a leading city (Tarsus). He was also a freeborn Roman citizen. In the Jewish society of his day, he was at the top of the tree.

In graphic language, Paul describes all these benefits as 'garbage', compared with knowing Christ (Philippians 3:7–8). So what was important to Paul in his new life? He wanted to close the gap between him and Christ: 'I press on towards the goal . . . ' (Philippians 3:14). This 'Hebrew of Hebrews' (3:5) now saw success in terms of knowing Christ and of finishing the course set for him.

Pause to think of those things in which you take greatest pride: your school, your university, your sporting achievements, your business success, your career, your social standing, even your family. A measure of your love for Christ is to ask yourself, 'If it came to a choice, which would I rather lose – all these things or my relationship with Jesus?'

In our thinking about success, we may find we are moulded much more by the attitudes and standards of this world than we care to admit. Perhaps, all too easily, we categorize people as 'winners and losers', 'successes and failures'. Could it be that, despite all our professed commitment to 'putting God first', we are actually driven by a desire for recognition, money, power and position? Maybe we have simply rationalized all this – it's simply the way things are in the world – and not allowed the Word of God to penetrate into this space in our lives. As part of the process of our minds being renewed by the Spirit of God (Romans 12:2), maybe our whole thinking about success needs to change.

Handling our own success

Very few people handle success well. When we are successful and receive praise from others, then we are most vulnerable to shifting into a fantasy world in which we start to believe that it is all down to us. We conveniently forget all the efforts of others in our overwhelming desire to capture all the adulation. There is also a great temptation to forget the God who made us, who gave us the brains, the skill and the energy, and who can take those things from us at any point. It is a sad irony that, in times of (seeming) success, the gap between us and God can actually widen because of our own sinful pride.

In Old Testament times, God warned his people repeatedly not to forget him in times of success and prosperity. Here is a sample from God's warning to Israel as they were about to enter the Promised Land:

> When the LORD your God brings you into the land he swore to your fathers . . . to give you – a land with large, flourishing cities you did not build, houses filled with all kinds of good things you did not provide, wells you did not dig, and vineyards and olive groves you did not plant – then when you eat and are satisfied, *be careful that you do not forget* the LORD, who brought you out of Egypt, out of the land of slavery. (Deuteronomy 6:10–12, italics mine)

The Old Testament shows that the people of Israel failed to heed this warning. They did forget. They became self-satisfied and complacent, as Moses had foreseen (Deuteronomy 32:15). They repeatedly forgot the Lord throughout their history, and failed to heed the warnings of the prophets who were sent to them (see, for example, Psalm 78). As a result, God took away the land and all its blessings from them (at least for a while), when the Babylonians carried them into captivity.

There is a warning here for us. When we enjoy success, the default response of our sinful human nature is to grab the credit and make sure everyone knows how well we have done and what good, clever, deserving people we are. We might then overlay this with a veneer of Christian spirituality, by saying that we are 'giving God the glory', but the underlying reality is that we are feeling rather proud, self-sufficient and self-satisfied. Superficially, we might remember to say 'thank you' to God, but in our hearts we have all but squeezed him out of the picture.

Success can also blind us to our own weaknesses. It makes us feel invulnerable, indispensable even. For an example of a successful leader on the world stage who completely 'lost it' in this sense, the Old Testament book of Daniel tells the story of King Nebuchadnezzar. As he looked around at the great riches and power of the kingdom he ruled, he uttered these unforgettable words: 'Is not this the great Babylon I have built as the royal residence, by my mighty power and for the glory of my majesty?' (Daniel 4:30). Note the use of 'I' and 'my'! I guess we can all think of political and business leaders and celebrities, whose self-centred view of their success is in the same category, whose inflated ego leads them to regard others as lesser beings.

Maybe you know some 'mini-Nebuchadnezzars' where you work. Perhaps you are one yourself! Those who calmly, and seemingly without any qualms, claim the sole credit for any success, who take every opportunity to promote the cult of their own personality. Watch how some people's behaviour changes in this regard when they are promoted; notice how they start to speak, dress and behave differently. Maybe you have fallen into this trap, mentally rewriting history to minimize the efforts of others and convincing yourself that *you* are really the key to it all. It's not attractive behaviour. Surely, God isn't much impressed by this sort of posturing.

Look around the world today. It's not difficult to identify many leaders in public life, even in the church, who cling on to office in the misguided belief that they alone can lead and no-one else can do the job as well as they can. If you hold a leadership position, beware of ever thinking of yourself as indispensable. A work colleague, with a wicked sense of humour, once suggested that I should apply the 'indispensability test': 'Put your hand in a bucket of water,' he suggested. 'When you take it out, then the size of the hole you leave indicates how indispensable you are.'

Success can blind us to our weaknesses and give us an inflated sense of our own importance. It can also distort our values when we start to get things out of proportion and set store by the short-lived trappings of success at the expense of our relationships with others and with God.

When God gives us success, let's enjoy the moment. Let's thank God with a whole heart, and acknowledge in our celebration all those who have contributed to it.

Handling success in others

The Scriptures call us to 'Rejoice with those who rejoice; mourn with those who mourn' (Romans 12:15). Most of us don't find it too hard to obey the second part of this command.

We may be easily moved to tears, to prayer and to loving sympathy by the distress of those we know. Perversely, we often find it much harder to 'rejoice with those who rejoice'. The extent to which we can do this reveals the measure of our love for those enjoying success when we are not. For example, few of us would find it difficult to derive great joy and satisfaction from the success of our children, a close friend or our marriage partner. It is much harder to celebrate the success of someone whom we see as our competitor in the game of life, whether a workmate or a sibling.

This is a common experience. Perhaps your work colleague is offered a promotion with a big pay rise, a promotion that you had wanted for yourself and thought you deserved, and you are left doing the same old job. Or your best mate announces his engagement to the most attractive, interesting girl you know, and you are left feeling lonely and left out. Or your brothers and sisters all seem to have secure jobs and plenty of money, while you are still desperately looking for work and have a zero bank balance. This sort of situation is often a serious test of our faith. Why doesn't God answer *my* prayers? Why is *she* so successful? Why not me?

Just as we are to pray for those we live and work with, including those whom we find difficult, and even our enemies, so we are to practise being thankful to God when he blesses them. Try doing this. It will move you out of the pit of self-obsession we sometimes wallow in, and you will be more in step with the Spirit of God.

A long-term view

We need a long-term view, an eternal view on success. Success as rated by most societies in this age can be short-lived, of no lasting value at all. God's time-frame for measuring success is eternity. The writer of Psalm 73 is at first puzzled as to why evil people seem to be so successful in the world, while honest people are often exploited and seem to miss out on the best in life. But as the psalm goes on, the writer starts to view things differently. He begins to see the seemingly successful ones who have taken the moral short cuts as God sees them – on a slippery downward slope, in a very dangerous position (Psalm 73:18). This glimpse into eternity changes the psalmist's view of success.

What successes are you striving for right now? Where are you investing your time and energy? Let's re-examine our priorities in the light of eternity, align our thinking about success with the Scriptures, and aim to live to please God. Let's make it our priority to be faithful to our particular calling, the work and the relationships with which God has entrusted us. When our time comes to die, I doubt we will be wishing we had worked harder and longer to get more money. The position we had done our utmost to attain will no longer look so important. Our most precious successes will not provide much comfort. So let's make sure we can look back with as few regrets as possible about the value of the things we have spent our lives working for, and the way we have used that most precious gift of God – our time.

Reflection

What success do you crave? Why?

In what ways is God calling you to be faithful and obedient?

Is there a particular task he is calling you to complete?

PART 4:
THE GAP IS CLOSED . . .
WHEN WE GROW THROUGH
TOUGH TIMES

9. Recovering from failure

Do not gloat over me, my enemy!
Though I have fallen, I will rise.
Though I sit in darkness,
the LORD will be my light.
(Micah 7:8)

The gap between the success we long for and what we actually achieve

'Failure is not an option' is written on the wall at my local gym. It's meant to motivate us to press on to achieve our fitness goals. But most of us do fail to achieve many of our goals – even in fitness. In life, failure isn't just an option; it's an experience we all have. How do we handle it? What difference does our Christian faith make when we fail?

As we saw in the last chapter, we need to learn to handle our successes and triumphs. We also need to learn to cope with our failures and disasters. Referring to triumphs and disasters, Rudyard Kipling's poem, 'If', encourages us to ' . . . treat these two imposters just the same'. But on the rollercoaster of life, that sort of equanimity is usually beyond us. Both success and failure are character building and test our faith, but in very different ways, and they bring out very different responses.

Most of us have low tolerance for failure . . . in others. 'You loser' is a common put-down. But we all fail in one way or another. The most successful world leader or business person may be a failure in her marriage, or with her children, or in her personal relationships. All of us fail at some time or other, in one way or another. We may prefer to brush our own failures under the carpet or wallow in self-pity, but we would be wiser to ask, 'What can I learn from my experience of failure? How do I recover from it? What does Scripture have to say to me? What good news does God have for me when I fail? How can I help others who are experiencing failure?'

Before we try to come up with some answers, let's consider what we mean by 'failure', its causes, and how it affects us.

What do we mean by failure?

We call it 'failure', *when we don't achieve what we want to achieve*. We will not always come out on top. We won't always get the promotion, win the tender, get the job we wanted or achieve our business goals. We may fail to live up to our own expectations or to perform to the level that others expect of us. Our employers, spouses and parents may place a heavier burden of expectation on us than we are able to bear.

The challenge for the Christian, in times of success and failure, is to be clear who it is that we are really working and living for. Is it for ourselves and our own glory, to keep other people happy, or for the Lord and to honour him?

We may also say we have failed *in not becoming the people we want to be*. You may have an image in your mind of the person you really want to be – strong, respected, faithful, honest, loving – but the reality somehow falls far short. For example, you may feel that you have failed in the relationships that matter to you most as a friend, a husband or wife, or as a parent. As a Christian, you may feel you fail to make a difference or have an impact on anyone's life for good. You read the biography of a great Christian leader which motivates and encourages you, but it may also leave you feeling hopelessly inadequate; you look at what the great man or woman in the book has achieved and by comparison you feel a failure.

Indeed, in our darker moments we may feel that we have achieved nothing worthwhile in our lives at all.

More importantly, we all fail *to be the people God wants us to be*. The Bible makes clear that God is more concerned with our faithfulness to him than with our personal goals and idealistic dreams. As we grow in our knowledge of God and are changed, as we put our faith and hope in him, as we build relationships that honour him and reflect his love for us, as our daily work becomes an integral part of our worship and as we commit ourselves to making a difference for good in this world, so the gaps are closed, bit by bit. But gaps will remain as long as we are on this earth, because the power of human sinfulness and evil is very strong. When we think we are flying high, we can quickly be brought crashing down to earth.

We may fail to achieve what we want to achieve, to become what we want to become, in our work, our marriage, our parenting or in our relationships generally. We can fail in just about every area of life that involves any effort or commitment on our part. We will most certainly fail to live up to God's standards and deliver on our promises to him. We are, after all, fallible human beings, and therefore prone to failure.

Many of our failures are caused by *our own moral weakness* when we compromise our standards, succumb to temptation and let ourselves and our family down. Some of our failures are *due to our own stupidity* (another manifestation of our sinfulness). We may fail an exam simply because we have neglected to study, or fail to get a job because we haven't prepared for the interview. And sometimes we fail simply *because we are not as good as the other guy*. Even after we have worked our hardest and prepared well, we still don't get the contract, the promotion or the job. That sort of failure is especially hard to take. Or sometimes we fail *due to circumstances entirely beyond our control*. Some major event, such as a flood, a fire or a stock market crash, may destroy all we have worked for and leave us asking why.

A painful experience

J. K. Rowling, the outstandingly successful author of the Harry Potter series, looking back on her experience before her books were published, said this:

> . . . by any conventional measure, a mere seven years after my graduation day I had failed on an epic scale, an exceptionally short-lived marriage had imploded, and I was jobless, a lone parent, and as poor as it is possible to be in modern Britain without being homeless . . . I am not going to stand here and tell you failure is fun. That period of my life was a dark one.[1]

Yes, failure has a dark side. Failure is usually painful, particularly when you have worked long and hard preparing a tender for a big contract that you don't win, when the small business that you have put your life savings into crashes, or when your job applications are rejected again and again.

How do you cope with failure? It depends to some extent on your personality and on your mood and circumstances at the time. Sometimes we might be able to shrug off failures as minor setbacks, redouble our efforts, look forward and press on. At other times, failure can hit like a body blow, leaving scars that take a long time to heal. If you are a parent, you may find it easier to cope with your own failures than those of your children.

Failure can bring shame on ourselves and our families, particularly when that failure is public, such as a moral failure relating to money or sex.

Failure may bring fear: fear of admitting your weakness to others. A Christian businessman I know lost his job as a finance manager. He asked a group of us to pray for him and he was able to get another job fairly quickly. But then he was made redundant again and he stopped attending the group. It turned out that he was ashamed that this had happened twice. He was fearful of being seen as a failure twice over, fearful of what others might think of him. He felt that he had somehow let the group down and let God down, and he was too ashamed to come back and ask for prayer again – as though God could not answer his prayers a second time.

Failure may leave us feeling that we are of no value. Ask yourself, 'Is my self-esteem and my estimate of my worth as a human being based on what I have achieved, or on my relationship to God?' If it is the former, then we have a problem: what happens when we fail?

Failure is usually a painful experience, which tests our faith in our heavenly Father. But it can also be a learning experience.

What can we learn from failure?

First, *we need to keep learning from Scripture*. The Bible mirrors real life and is full of human failure, particularly moral failure. Right from the beginning, Adam and Eve failed to obey the simplest instruction; they failed to pass the test. Cain failed to love his brother, and murdered him out of jealousy. Abraham failed the honesty test when he tried to pass his wife off as his sister in the Egyptian court. Moses, Gideon, Samson, even Elijah, all the great heroes of the faith, failed in different ways consistently to trust and obey God.

Psalm 78 looks back over the history of God's people and sees a recurring pattern of failure to keep God's covenant, to be the people he had called them to be and even to remember God at all. Certainly, any failures in our lives are not going to take God by surprise!

Second, *we can learn from our own mistakes*, when we just don't handle situations well. In the delightful film *Groundhog Day*, the main character, played by Bill Murray, is repeatedly given the opportunity to relive his daily encounters. Each time he handles the situations better, as he learns from his mistakes. Some days, when we come home from work, we might love to have a groundhog day – a real-time rerun.

In real life, however, we don't get to *relive* our mistakes; but we do have the opportunity to learn from them.

Third, failure doesn't just provide the opportunity to learn to 'do it better next time'. When we fail, *we learn more about ourselves*, our weaknesses, our values and our motivation. Knute Rockne, widely regarded as the best coach in the history of American college football, said this: 'The way a man wins shows much of his character and the way he loses shows all of it.' Wayne Bennett, the great Australian Rugby League coach, used to say that he and his team always learned a lot more about themselves from a loss than from a big victory.

Failure has a way of bringing us back from fantasy land to face the truth about ourselves: to learn that we are not quite as good as we thought and that we need to lift our game to achieve our goals.

We can also learn from *others* who seem to have failed and yet have battled on through adversity to eventual success. Recently I had the opportunity to visit Robben Island, the site of the former notorious jail off the coast of South Africa, near Cape Town. Nelson Mandela spent eighteen of his twenty-seven years of imprisonment there. Breaking rocks in the quarry all day, in the glare of the African sun (which permanently damaged his eyesight), he must have experienced many low points, when it seemed that he had failed completely to achieve his lifelong goals. But as we now know, the great man survived this long ordeal and emerged as the victorious leader of the new South Africa.

Failure can be a great teacher. We can learn a lot from failure – our own, and that of others.

God knows we will often fail – to achieve our own goals, to become the people we would like to be, or to be the people he calls us to be. After all,

> He knows how we are formed,
> he remembers that we are dust.
> (Psalm 103:14)

But God does not intend us to wallow in our failures. He surely means us to face them, to learn from them, to grow through them and to press on, and that takes commitment on our part, as well as daily reliance on the strengthening of the Holy Spirit of God.

The struggle

When I lived in East Africa, I was able to climb Mount Kilimanjaro on two occasions. It is a beautiful mountain, but ascending the last thousand metres involves a steady struggle up a steep slope of volcanic ash, at an altitude of over 5,000 metres. My memory is of climbing two steps forward and then sliding back. Sometimes that is how the Christian life feels: two steps forward, one step back, or sometimes, in a quite humbling way, one step forward and a great slide back. We get a fresh glimpse of the reality of God and then somehow lose sight of him again. We might wonder if we are making any progress at all, and feel like giving up altogether. The Bible term for having our lives changed by the power of God is 'sanctification', a process which one Christian writer, J. A. Motyer, called 'progressive victory at cost'. Certainly that's how climbing Kilimanjaro felt!

When Paul wanted to describe the Christian life to his young protégé Timothy, he illustrated it in terms of an athlete who has to train, a farmer who has to work and a soldier who has to fight (see 2 Timothy 2).

Or to use a different analogy, it can feel like playing snakes and ladders (chutes and ladders, if you come from North America). Sometimes we feel as if we have climbed a ladder and can see the world from a higher vantage point, only to slide down the snakes, back to where we started – or worse. As I go through life, I find that I continually have to face tests and challenges to my faith that I thought I had dealt with years before. It leaves me wondering if I have made any progress at all as a professing Christian.

But as I look back over my own life and share the experience of others, it seems to me that a more accurate picture than the chancy business of snakes and ladders is a spiral staircase. Seen from above, someone climbing a spiral staircase looks as if he is going round in circles, always coming back to the same point. In reality, of course, he is steadily climbing to a higher point.

So on the occasions when it *seems* like we have slipped back to the same point, that is not in fact the case. How can we be at the *same* point, when time and life have moved on and we have become different people through the cumulative effect of our experiences and the decisions and actions we have taken? Let's look at 'failure' and setbacks differently: not as sliding back to where we were, but as having to relearn the same lessons *at a higher level*, further up the spiral staircase, closer to our final destination.

The fight

As we understand what Christ has done for us and commit ourselves to cooperating with the Holy Spirit's work in our lives, we start to confront a less comfortable truth: we find ourselves not just in a struggle, but in a spiritual war zone. In our commitment to live close to God in our daily experience and make a difference in the world, we struggle against more than just inanimate elements, like running into a headwind or climbing a steep mountain. We battle against an active opponent. Actually, the Bible tells us that opposition comes from three sources, which are separate, but interlinked. No wonder we fail or suffer defeats from time to time, particularly when we either forget or underestimate the forces ranged against us.

First, there is the *weakness of our own human nature*. We are our own worst enemy. Our natural tendency is always to put ourselves, our pride and our desires above anyone or anything else. But when God's Spirit enters our life, his agenda is to change us. Our lives become a battleground in which the Spirit is striving to overcome our human weakness. Paul describes this in his letter to the Galatians: 'For the flesh desires what is contrary to the Spirit, and the Spirit what is contrary to the flesh. They are in conflict with each other, so that you do not do what you want' (5:17–18). How can we win this battle? Paul tells us, 'So I say, live by the Spirit, and you will not gratify the desires of the flesh' (5:16). It is a day-by-day, hour-by-hour and moment-by-moment fight.

We also experience *opposition from the godless society in which we live*, sometimes referred to in the Bible as 'the world'. Peer pressure doesn't end with teenage years; there is pressure throughout life to conform to the views and standards of society, rather than live to please God. That's why the Bible has to warn us, 'Do not love the world or anything in the world . . . For everything in the world – the lust of the flesh, the lust of the eyes, and the pride of life – comes not from the Father but from the world . . . The world and its desires pass away' (1 John 2:15–17), and 'Do not conform to the pattern of this world' (Romans 12:1). Rather, we are called to make a difference in the world for good, as Christ did.

Behind all the opposition we experience, both from within ourselves and from the world, there exists the personification of evil, the devil himself. Of course, the devil is not taken seriously in most circles. He is depicted as a pantomime figure.

> The devil has been voted out; the devil's dead and gone,
> But some of us would like to know, who carries his business on.
> (anon.)

The power of evil in this world is sometimes overwhelming: the child abuse, the pointless stabbings, muggings and murders of innocent people on our city streets, the brutal dictatorships, the exploitation and neglect of the poor, the hidden atrocities committed in secret police cells in so many countries. There are indeed dark forces at work. We can ignore them for a while, but eventually they will surface and impact on our lives. When life in a seemingly peaceful place is shattered when two ten-year-old children murder a younger child, or when someone goes berserk in a schoolyard with an automatic weapon, evil is exposed as a powerful, destructive force.

Evil is real. Jesus took the devil very seriously, and so should we. He was tempted by the devil in the wilderness (Matthew 4), and tempted to avoid suffering when his friend Peter suggested an easier way than death on a cross (Matthew 16:23). Jesus' prayers in the garden of Gethsemane on the night before his death reveal his deep spiritual struggle (Matthew 26:36–44).

Finally, on the cross Jesus fought the powers of darkness and won. He taught his disciples to pray each day: 'Deliver us from the evil one' (Matthew 6:13). On the night before his death, he prayed for his disciples that his Father would ' . . . protect them from the evil one' (John 17:15). The whole purpose of Jesus' life and death is described by the apostle John as ' . . . to destroy the devil's work' (1 John 3:8).

The crucial battle with evil was fought and won by Jesus, but the devil is still very dangerous. He is like a wounded animal on the prowl (1 Peter 5:8). We have to be ready to fight him. Each day we need to be 'very careful . . . how [we] live, because the days are evil' (Ephesians 5:15–16). That is, we don't go out to work or school or into a society which is neutral. We go out into enemy territory, however attractively it is dressed. Our fight is not with people ('Our struggle is not against flesh and blood', Ephesians 6:12), but with the devil and his spiritual forces. The same devil who tempted Jesus to give up is a foe to be taken seriously.

One of the most useful books for people just setting out on the Christian life was written in the 1970s by the Canadian psychiatrist John White. His book, *The Fight*, has recently been reprinted. Unlike many other books of that time and since, it does not present an 'airy-fairy' view of Christian experience as a cruise through life, enjoying health, success and all the goodies on offer. Rather, it presents the true biblical picture – that we had better get ready for a long fight.

Yes, it is a fight. Temptation is very strong. Under the combined pressure of 'the world, the flesh and the devil', we quickly fall and fail, and go back to our old ways of thinking and behaving. We continually need the forgiving grace of God, the renewing grace of God and the strengthening grace of God to go out and fight another day.

I love the words of the prophet Micah, who clearly knew this experience:

> Do not gloat over me, my enemy!
>   Though I have fallen, I will rise.
> Though I sit in darkness,
>   the LORD will be my light.
> (Micah 7:8)

The Bible calls us to clothe ourselves with 'the whole armour of God' (Ephesians 6). Paul clearly has a picture in his mind of a Roman soldier ready for battle. The modern equivalent would be a police officer in full riot gear. We are to put on truth, which holds us firmly like a belt; the breastplate of righteousness, the knowledge that God has credited his righteousness to us; and shoes, so that we are ready to go out with the good news of what God has done.

We need to take up the shield of faith to protect us from the fears and doubts that may bombard us, those doubts that flood in when life gets hard; the helmet of salvation (the daily reminder that God has saved us); and the 'sword of the Spirit, which is the word of God'.

Non-Christians see the Bible as just another religious book, and sceptics regard it as merely the fabrication of the church. But the Christian, whose life has been changed by the power of its truth, knows it to be a revelation of God and a powerful God-given weapon in the battle between good and evil.

Recovery from failure

Sometimes the struggle is too much for us. Sometimes the enemy is too strong and we fail, morally and spiritually, and feel miserable about it. The Bible is full of people who have failed, and of examples of the grace of God in forgiving, renewing and restoring such people.

Think of the public failure of Peter, the man who had vowed never to desert Jesus, but then denied even knowing him, and at the time of Jesus' greatest need (Matthew 26:69–75). However familiar you are with the story, it is still astonishing.

But even more astonishing is Jesus' equally clear forgiveness and restoration of Peter when they met on the shore of Lake Galilee after Jesus' resurrection (John 21:15–19). Peter, who became a great leader of the church, has been known for two thousand years as the one who let Jesus down! Think about that and you catch a glimpse of the grace of God that enabled Peter not to shrink away in embarrassment because of the 'failure tag' forever hung around his neck, but rather to stand up in public and speak out boldly for Jesus Christ. When the Holy Spirit came at Pentecost, all Peter's past failure was no longer a constraint.

The key to how he was able to 'live with himself', as we would say, after such a humiliating failure is that, like Paul, he understood that ' . . . what we preach is not ourselves, but Jesus Christ as Lord, and ourselves as your servants for Jesus' sake' (2 Corinthians 4:5). Peter could face anyone and say in effect, 'Yes, I was a great failure, and I am capable of failing again, but let me tell you not about me, but about Jesus Christ who died for me.' That is why the gospel is liberating.

After letting Jesus down *so* badly, Peter must have felt that Jesus could not use him again, that he was no longer worthy and could not be trusted. And yet, Jesus gave him a job to do:

three times Jesus reassured Peter that he still loved him and that he was to take on a new role: to become a shepherd leader of the early church.

If you feel you have failed, then maybe God has a new direction for you to take, a new role, a new job in a new location; or maybe God wants you to stay right where you are, to learn from that failure and press on. Perhaps God wants a new person in your situation . . . but that person is you. Let's never exclude people from fellowship, or from opportunities for service, just because they have failed. Jesus didn't.

Or think about examples of moral failure. King David was a man of faith, the author of many of the Psalms, the hero who had stood up to Goliath. But later in life, when he had become king, he succumbed dramatically to sexual temptation and slept with another man's wife. In attempting to cover up what he knew to be wrong, he then compounded his sin by sending her husband to the battle front where, sure enough, he was killed, just as David had planned.

The prophet Nathan courageously confronted David with his double crime of adultery and murder, and with the exploitation of his kingly power. David broke down and turned to God in repentance (see 2 Samuel 11 – 12). The consequences of David's actions continued to cause problems for him and his family right to the end of his life, despite his seeking and receiving God's forgiveness (Psalm 51).

So these great biblical heroes, Peter and David (we could mention many others), failed at crucial times to be the people they wanted to be and, more importantly, failed to be the people God had called them to be. Both learned painful lessons about their own weakness and valuable lessons about God's great grace in the process. The whole history of the people of Israel in the Old Testament seems to be one of recurring failure to remember what God had done for them, failure to trust him to guide, protect and provide for them, and failure to be faithful to him. Yet, despite their many failures, we see the grace of God at work, forgiving and renewing them.

When I was in my twenties and had just become a Christian, I thought a lot about whether God could lift my quality of life permanently on to a higher plane. Was there some great experience I could have, as many claim, that would change me once and for all so that sin and temptation would no longer be a problem?

At that time I heard the late Alan Redpath speak at a Christian conference. He began by asking the question: 'What does God expect of you?' Leading us to think of possible answers, maybe to serve him, to be a better person, to become a great leader, Dr Redpath then answered his own question with these surprising words: 'God expects nothing of you but failure . . . but he has given you his Holy Spirit that you need not fail.' He went on to say that God knows what we are like inside, and we can't pretend to him. In the penetrating words of Psalm 139:

> You know when I sit and when I rise;
>> you perceive my thoughts from afar.
> You discern my going out and my lying down;
>> you are familiar with all my ways.
> (verses 2–3)

God knows all our weaknesses and strengths. He knows our personality; he made us. That's why faith and worship must begin with honesty: an honest assessment of our situation, our problems and our need, in the light of God's truth.

God expects nothing of us but failure in our own efforts to lift our standards. But he has given us his Holy Spirit that we need not fail. As day by day and moment by moment we rely on God, on his grace, power and direction, so we are changed: we climb the spiral staircase, we experience a closing of the gap in this life, and know 'the goodness of the LORD in the land of the living' (Psalm 27:13). And as we keep close to Christ, continue to read God's Word and rely on the help of his Spirit, rather than on our own resources, we will come through our many experiences of failure stronger and wiser.

Practical steps

Both David and Peter failed and then recovered. Of course, it's much easier to talk about failures *after* you have recovered from them. But what if you are actually going through an experience of failure right now?

When a business is failing or a sports team loses, the leader's response is often to 'go back to basics', 'back to the drawing board'. That's usually good advice and it also applies, I believe, to the Christian in situations of failure. If you feel you have failed in what you want to achieve, failed to become what you wanted to be, or if you are carrying a load of guilt because you have failed God, then go back to basics. Here are seven steps forward in recovering from failure, whether dealing with our own failures or encouraging and supporting someone else experiencing failure.

1. **Rediscover your value in the sight of God**. According to the Bible, the value of our life, our worth, is *not* measured by what we have achieved, by the wealth we have accumulated (our net assets), or by our title, qualifications and status in society. No, it is the value God has put on our life in giving his Son for us – we have been redeemed with the precious blood of Christ. That is how much you are worth to God, whatever you achieve or fail to achieve. That is value that lasts.

2. **Focus on Christ**, on his great love for you and his grace, rather than on yourself and your shortcomings: the Bible calls us to consider him, to learn from him, to be rooted and grounded in him, to remain in him, to please him. We can't please everybody, so we are to make it our aim to please Christ: that simplifies life a lot.

3. **Do the little things well**: Jesus said that we need to be faithful in the small things if we are to be trusted with bigger things. Do one thing well, some act of service, and take a step forward, rather than dwell on your failure.

4. **Resist the temptation to succumb to envy, jealousy and bitterness**, but rather be thankful. Thankfulness is an attractive quality; envy and jealousy are not.

5. **Invest time in relationships**, rather than in possessions and struggling for power. Learn to value people above things.

6. **Hold on and don't give up trusting** that God has a great plan for you. Sometimes that's the hardest thing, although an apparent failure may provide another opportunity to learn to trust.

7. **Press on and take whatever opportunities are open to you**. The apostle Paul suffered many setbacks and seeming failures in his life; he spent long years chained in a prison cell when he really wanted to be out travelling as an evangelist and building up churches, but he certainly didn't wallow in self-pity. He had '. . . learned the secret of being content in any and every situation' (Philippians 4:12). His faith had been tested through apparent failure to achieve what he wanted to achieve. In the same letter he also wrote, '. . . one thing I do: forgetting what is behind and straining towards what is ahead, I press on towards the goal' (3:13–14).

Sir Winston Churchill once said, 'Success is not final. Failure is not final. It is the courage to continue that counts.'

Reflection

Why do we fail to be the people we want to be?

Reflect on the many examples of 'failure' of God's people in the Bible (e.g. Peter, David). What can we learn from them?

Reflect also on the promises of God to restore 'failures'.

10. Tested faith

Though he slay me, yet will I hope in him.
(Job 13:15)

The gaps in our understanding of God

When things go wrong, we start to question God, to blame God (isn't he ultimately in control?) and to examine the basis of our faith in God. We see a gap between the God of love and power revealed in the Bible and his seeming failure to fix our problems.

Then the faith we have professed is tested. A gap opens up between what we have *said* we believe about God (and the way we have encouraged others to trust God) and the extent to which we really trust him when the going gets tough.

As I write this, there are major floods in the Philippines. Many have died, and thousands more have lost their homes and possessions. A distraught fifteen-year-old girl was interviewed on a twenty-four-hour news channel: 'We love Jesus,' she said, 'so why this?'

Every generation struggles with the gap between how we think God should behave and what actually happens. In her moving book, *The Two of Us*, Sheila Hancock shares her emotional anguish in having to watch her husband, the actor John Thaw, slowly die of cancer. Reflecting on her husband's suffering, and the appalling suffering in the world generally, she voices feelings that many of us would echo: 'And some people believe in a merciful God. Well, he's not very good at his job, that's all I can say.'[1]

Even those who have so far come through life relatively unscathed by personal tragedy may feel disappointed with their lot, with their circumstances and accomplishments. They may feel there is a gap between what was advertised and what was delivered, as if God made a promise he cannot or will not honour. Many transfer their disappointment with their life into blame of God: he has failed to deliver. What reason could there be for me to be interested in him? Why should I trust him?

In one way or another our faith will be tested, whether in the crisis times of pain and bereavement or in the day-to-day pressures of life. It is in learning to trust God through those testing times that we grow in our knowledge of God; our faith deepens, and becomes lasting and transforming.

Big issues – big questions

A few years ago I was busy repainting the bedroom at home. I was listening to a radio interview with Michael Parkinson, the well-known TV personality. He was asked if he was religious. 'No,' he replied. 'When you've seen some of the suffering in the world that I've seen in my years in national service in the army, and as a war correspondent, you find it very hard to believe in a God of love or a God of justice.' At that point, I stopped and put down my paintbrush.

It was Good Friday, the day when Christians around the world remember the torture and death of the man Jesus, whom Christians believe to be the Son of God. What irony in hearing these words on *that* day of all days. According to

Scripture, on the first Good Friday, 'God was reconciling the world to himself in Christ' (2 Corinthians 5:19). When Jesus died, God was not watching dispassionately, as yet another innocent man suffered cruelly. God was involved in the person of his Son. He himself suffered. To use the words of Bette Midler's song, he was not watching 'from a distance'. Some theologians object to the idea that the unchangeable God can be said to suffer pain. But if Jesus is indeed divine as well as human, then he does. As D. A. Carson observes, 'The God on whom we rely knows what suffering is all about, not merely in the way that God knows everything, but by experience.'[2]

I have a copy of the script of *The Sign of Jonah*, a play written after the Second World War by Günter Rutenborn. The drama is set in a courtroom, where blame was to be apportioned and sentence passed on those responsible for the murder of 5 million Jews, the collapse of the German state, the destruction of its cities and the deaths of millions of soldiers and civilians. Who was to blame? Was it the country's leaders, the political system, or the 'man in the street' who was content to let it all happen around him?

In the end, everyone comes to the same conclusion: God is guilty! He is ultimately responsible. What sentence should be passed on him?

'Well,' says the 'man in the street' who has lost his wife and children and home in the war, 'he must spend a human lifetime on this earth, just like myself. He must be forced to wander about without having a home. He is to feel the pain of what it means to lose a son. Give him a son . . . let him suffer hunger, thirst and the agony of death, just like myself. Perhaps then he will govern future centuries more wisely.'

The woman adds her sentence: 'He shall be born of a woman, on the road, and the misery of tortured creation shall pierce his ears day and night. The sick, marked by leprosy and nausea, shall surround him: he shall have to look on stinking corpses; yes, he himself shall lose a son.'

The judge then sums up: 'Bring him, then, the sentence laid upon him by tortured mankind. Condemn him to the hellish journey of being Man.' Gabriel, the angel at the judge's right hand, volunteers, 'I, Gabriel, shall go to a virgin by the name of Mary. She shall bear him . . . as a Jew.'[3]

The play leaves us to ponder these two great biblical truths. God is in control, and he knows what it is to suffer. Indeed, he experienced suffering himself through the life and death of his Son. Yet it still leaves us asking why.

Christians have struggled for centuries with this problem, spiritually, emotionally and intellectually. If God is all-loving, all-knowing and all-just, then surely he would end all injustice and suffering. So why does he not do so?

It would be both foolish and presumptuous to attempt to deal with such a huge issue of faith in these few pages. But we can consider the way in which adverse circumstances and personal crises challenge our understanding of God and test our faith in him.[4]

The test of not knowing

A friend of mine, who watched his mother die of cancer, asked me, 'What does your church tell you to say to people in this situation?' He thought Christians pulled out a pat answer like a library book from the shelf. Of course, there is no explanation available to us in this life that fully answers our questions.

The Bible also poses some questions. Many of the Old Testament Psalms ask God specifically why the wicked seem to prosper and innocent people suffer (e.g. Psalm 73). No simple answer comes back. We know that God uses suffering to grow character (Romans 5:4–5), by disciplining us as a father disciplines his children (Hebrews 12:7), and in testing and purifying our faith (1 Peter 1:7). We have his promise that 'in all things God works for the good of those who love him' (Romans 8:28). We also know that many things may happen that we simply don't understand, because he is God and we are not. As Isaiah reminds us,

> Who can fathom the Spirit of the LORD,
>   or instruct the LORD as his counsellor?
> (Isaiah 40:13)

However, in any particular situation, it may be far from clear just how things are working for our good, when the outlook seems all bad. It may be difficult to see why God planned or allowed certain circumstances. The link between cause and effect is often too complicated for us. We don't know, we don't understand, and we struggle to reconcile what we know of God with our experience. So our faith is tested.

As D. A. Carson observes,

> It is the uncertainty of reading what is going on that sometimes breeds pain. Is the particular blow I am facing God's way of telling me to change something? Or is it a form of discipline designed to toughen me or soften me to make me more useful? Or is it part of the heritage of all sons and daughters of Adam who live this side of the parousia, unrelated to discipline but part of God's mysterious providence in a fallen world?[5]

It is not our role to defend God or to justify his ways to other people. We don't have the knowledge or wisdom to unravel all the complexities, and we will simply make fools of ourselves if we try, as did Job's 'comforters'.

Despite these limitations, some Christian preachers, writers and counsellors can't seem to help themselves from claiming divine insight into God's specific intention in a situation, and dispensing their advice and wisdom.

Let's be very careful here. Remember that Job's friends thought they were defending God and helping Job, but in the end God accused *them* of misrepresenting him. There is a gap in our understanding which won't be closed until we see him. Until that day, we have to live in this life with many bewildering uncertainties as to why some things happen. That is often a huge test of our faith and patience.

Job provides a wonderful example of trusting God. He lost everything. His faith was stretched nearly to breaking point. Understandably, his suffering caused him to ask what he had done to deserve such troubles, after years of seeking to live a good life. 'Though he slay me, yet will I hope in him' (Job 13:15) were his final words on the issue of trust.

Please God we won't have to suffer as Job did, but we can certainly expect to have our faith tested. We had some friends who left the USA with their four daughters to lead a church on the French island of La Réunion in the Indian Ocean. From the moment they decided to go, things went wrong. Obtaining visas was a struggle, paperwork got lost, their plane tickets had not been paid. Nevertheless, they pressed on. The last straw was when my friend went down to the docks in Florida to find that all their crates of possessions had been lost in transit! If they were sacrificing the comforts and familiarity of home to do God's will, why was it so hard? Why didn't God smooth the way for them?

It was at that moment, my friend told me, that he remembered Job's words and applied them to his own situation. He reaffirmed his commitment to trust God, no matter what happened, and that was a turning point.

They found their way to La Réunion, their possessions eventually arrived safely, and they went on to live and work there successfully for many years. Sometimes all that remains is to trust in the promises of God.

> Many are the woes of the wicked,
>> but the LORD's unfailing love
>> surrounds the one who trusts in him.
> (Psalm 32:10)

Faith = trust

Sometimes the Christian faith is made to seem difficult and complicated. Our thinking gets confused; we lose sight of the simple and obvious and become bogged down in trivial issues which obscure the big picture.

As we have seen, there is often a gap between what *we say* we believe and how we behave. The core of Christianity is that we can have a relationship with God through Jesus Christ, a relationship based on *trust*.

It is all about trust: trust in a person, not belief in a concept, a creed or a theological system. There is a world of difference between saying, 'I believe in God', and being able to assert, 'I trust God.' The first statement does not require commitment. It need not influence the way we live. It may be just an interesting topic for discussion over a cup of coffee.

The second statement, though, involves a commitment to a relationship, with huge implications for the way we live. It is easy to say, 'I believe in God, or in a god.' The question that really matters is: 'Do you trust him?' And further, 'In what ways do you trust him? How much do you trust him?'

Trust is the basis of any successful relationship. Friends trust each other with confidences, and to help one another. Married couples trust each other to keep their vows, and to protect and support each other. Business partners trust one another to deal honestly and work together for their mutual benefit.

But when trust is broken, then the lawyers, courts, social workers, police and sometimes prisons have to pick up the pieces. Trust is the basis of a free society.

Trust is essential for us to function in life. When we board an aircraft, we trust the pilot and air traffic controllers. We trust that the engineers have done their work and that the instruments are correct. We trust other drivers to stay on their side of the road and behave predictably when they hurtle towards us at 100 kph. Generally, we trust the advice we receive from medical experts. We entrust our children to schoolteachers for their formal education.

Trust is also the basis of our relationship with God, and much more so than in a human relationship, because we are trusting someone we cannot see. The Bible encourages us to trust God, to trust *in* him and in his Son Jesus Christ, particularly in situations when that trust is tested.

The Psalms give us many examples of trust in God in the struggles of life. We are called to trust God in times of fear:

> When I am afraid, I put my trust in you.
>> In God, whose word I praise –
> In God I trust and am not afraid.
>> What can mere mortals do to me?
> (Psalm 56:3–4)

When we are doubting, we are to trust for evidence of God's love:

Let the morning bring me word of your unfailing love,
>   for I have put my trust in you.
(Psalm 143:8)

Worries about the future direction of our lives may crowd into our minds, but we are called to trust God:

Commit your way to the LORD;
>   trust in him and he will do this.
(Psalm 37:5)

When we find ourselves struggling spiritually, we are to trust God:

Trust in him at all times, you people;
>   pour out your hearts to him,
>   for God is our refuge.
(Psalm 62:8)

When we face opposition, we are to trust God:

In you, LORD my God,
>   I put my trust.
I trust in you;
>   do not let me be put to shame,
>   nor let my enemies triumph over me.
(Psalm 25:1–2)

When it appears as though injustice is winning and evil people are unchecked, we are to trust God:

Do not fret because of those who are evil
>   or be envious of those who do wrong;

for like the grass they will soon wither.
(Psalm 37:1–2)

The Old Testament frequently contrasts trusting God with trusting in *someone* else (ourselves or political leaders, for instance), or in *something* else (such as in our religious experiences, astrology or spiritism). People in our society implicitly trust themselves, their governments, their trading and financial systems (at least until the 2008 global financial crisis!).

We rely on expert advice in many fields. That's fine, but we are to trust God and his Word first and foremost. We are called to trust in God rather than in powerful leaders:

It is better to take refuge in the LORD
    than to trust in princes.
(Psalm 118:9)

It is better to trust in the Lord rather than in our own wisdom:

Trust in the LORD with all your heart
    and lean not on your own understanding;
in all your ways submit to him,
    and he will make your paths straight.
(Proverbs 3:5–6)

We are to trust in God rather than in our own resources to fix problems:

Some trust in chariots and some in horses,
    but we trust in the name of the LORD our God.
(Psalm 20:7)

The prophet Isaiah warned the people, 'When someone tells you to consult mediums and spiritists, who whisper and mutter, should not a people enquire of their God? Why consult the dead on behalf of the living?'(Isaiah 8:19). Sometimes we are called to trust when there seems to be no good reason to do so. Our trust is often tested.

Faith in 'the stuff' of life

God calls us to trust him for our life partner, for health, in our work, for our children and for the future. In the late 1980s we were happily settled, living and working in Tasmania. But then the company I was working for was taken over, and we were confronted with a choice: either to stay in Tasmania or move to mainland Australia.

From a human perspective, it was not a good time to move. It meant uprooting our three children from their schools and friendships, and a major change for us all. As we weighed the pros and cons and prayed over the right thing to do, I read a book on guidance by Elisabeth Elliot, *God's Guidance: A Slow and Certain Light*.[6] Her advice, based on her own experience, jolted me out of my complacency. She suggested that, if you are faced with a choice between two paths which both seem equally good, choose the harder path, because it will strengthen your faith.

I don't think I have ever seen that advice stated so clearly in any of the many books written about guidance, but it is wise. Faith is not like elastic that can be suddenly stretched. Faith is like muscle, which grows stronger the more it is exercised. After we had decided to move, which seemed at the time to be the more difficult option, I read a poem by John Newton, the eighteenth-century slave trader who was converted to Christ:

Though troubles assail,
And dangers affright;
Though friends should all fail,
And foes all unite,
Yet one thing secures us
Whatever betide:
The Scripture assures us,
'The Lord will provide.'[7]

The Lord will provide. Those words encouraged us to move forward, trusting God to enable us to meet all the challenges and to provide everything our children needed.

Trust needs to be applied in all the day-to-day areas of life. If we cannot trust God during testing times, then how real is our faith? When we do trust God and move forward with him, our faith is strengthened, our religion becomes real in everyday life, and the gap between belief and behaviour is closed.

A Bible translator was searching for a word in a tribal language to represent what the Scriptures mean by believing in Christ and trusting Christ. Standing with a local villager one day, he pointed to an old man who was leaning heavily on his walking stick. 'What is he doing?' asked the translator. His friend gave him the word in the local language, and that was the word he later used in his translation. Truly, to trust Jesus means to lean all our weight upon him: not to have a bet each way on whether or not he is real, not to tack a bit of religion on to our secular lives, but to trust him as our Saviour, guide and friend. He calls us to trust him completely in life and in death, in success and in trouble, and that involves commitment.

When my wife and I got married, we lived for several years in the beautiful island of Mauritius. A group of friends used to meet in our home for Bible study. One of them confessed one night, 'I can believe all these things in my head. But I don't know how to experience them in my heart.'

One wise friend replied, 'I can give you the answer in one word: Obey! Do what God is telling you to do!' Willingness to commit to obeying Christ is the great test of whether we truly trust him.

Trust is very practical. We moved to live in Dubai about three years ago. Setting up a new home, in a new place, far away from friends and family, we had to relearn some lessons we thought we had learned long ago: lessons about trusting God for basic things, such as guidance, help and wisdom. We had to learn again to look to God each day and to trust that, as we claimed to believe, he is a loving Father. We have seen on so many occasions that it is when God moves us out of our comfort zone and gives us a new challenge that we actually start to trust him and be real in our faith.

When we first arrived in Dubai and started to attend a church here, we were reminded of Abraham and his faith. Abraham trusted God for his life, his family and his future. He left the comfort and security of his home and journeyed over to Egypt and back to the Promised Land. In the large expatriate population here in Dubai, many of us can identify with that. It is good for us to have our faith tested, to move out of our comfort zone, without our support networks and familiar things and places. Whether we like it or not, life is an uncertain and transient affair.

Even if we fight that and cling tightly to what is familiar by putting down roots in one location, we will eventually find that our sense of permanence will prove to be illusory. Children will grow up and move away. Old age will come all too quickly. We will lose many friends. We may have to move from the home to which we have clung. Everything we have relied on for security in life will eventually be taken away. Death will have the last word. Our best efforts to create security for ourselves in this life without God will fail. Surely, then, it is wiser to trust God from the start in all these things and to make him our security.

Trust and worry

In our society many of us live in a state of perpetual anxiety, which diminishes our quality of life.

Worry is the interest we pay on trouble *before* it comes. A Swedish proverb tells us: 'Worry makes a small thing cast a long shadow.' It is destructive and unproductive. But if God is our heavenly Father who loves us and can supply all our needs, and if we say we trust him, why then do we continue to worry? This gets to the heart of things.

For much of the time we are full of worry and anxiety, professing on the one hand to believe in God the Father, but not prepared to trust him in the practical day-to-day issues: work, money, health, relationships. No wonder there is a sense of unreality in our life, and the way others see our faith, if we do not actually trust the God in whom we claim to believe.

In the New Testament Jesus underlined the fact that we can trust God for *daily needs*. He contrasts trust in God with worry and anxiety:

> Therefore I tell you, do not worry about your life, what you will eat or drink; or about your body, what you will wear. Is not life more than food, and the body more than clothes? . . . Can any one of you by worrying add a single hour to your life? . . . So do not worry, saying, 'What shall we eat?' or 'What shall we drink?' or 'What shall we wear?' For the pagans run after all these things, and your heavenly Father knows that you

need them. But seek first his kingdom and his righteousness, and all these things will be given to you as well.
(Matthew 6:25–33)

Jesus goes on to give us several reasons why we should trust God and not worry. First, worrying will not lengthen our lives. Second, he reminds us that, if God looks after the flowers of the field and the birds of the air, won't he, much more, look after us? Third, if we, who profess to be Christians, are as worried as our non-Christian friends, then our faith is shown to be quite shallow.

Of course, it is much easier for me to write these words than to stop worrying. Let me confess to having spent many a sleepless night beset by worry. As you lie awake, feeling unwell at 3 am, even little problems start to take on massive proportions. We may not be able to stop worries crowding into our minds, but we can decide how to deal with them. We can turn them into prayers; we can read and meditate on the promises of God; and, very importantly, we can remind ourselves of how God has brought us through many worrying times in the past. This was what the psalmists clearly did, and what God's faithful people have done for generations (see, for example, Psalm 40).

Let's make sure that our worries drive us *towards* God, not *away from* him. Worries may provide a daily test of our faith, but they also provide a daily opportunity to trust God and draw closer to him.

Life and death

So the Bible calls us to trust God rather than ourselves; to trust in him rather than in the stars, the spirits, the wisdom of this world or in anything else. Jesus reminds us that we are to trust, rather than be anxious in the day-to-day rough and tumble of life. But Jesus also talks about trusting God in the life-and-death issues.

On the night before his death, Jesus shared some of his most precious teaching with his closest friends. As he faced death, the ultimate test of faith, he said to his friends, 'Do not let your hearts be troubled. You believe in God; believe also in me' (John 14:1). Jesus spoke these words at a time when he himself had good cause to be overwhelmed with fear and anxiety. But with his amazing concern for others, his focus was more on his disciples and their worries.

He calls them to trust in him, as their faith faces the great test of seeing their beloved leader publicly humiliated and cruelly killed. He calls them (and us) to trust that he knows what he is doing (John 13:7); that he knows where he is going, back to his Father (13:33, 36); that he will not leave them (14:18); that one day they will be reunited (14:3); that he will not let them fall away (17:11); that Jesus truly is who he claims to be (14:8–9); and that he is in control (14:1). To learn to trust Jesus like that is to find the peace which the world cannot give or take away, as he promised (John 16:33).

There are many questions that will not be answered in this life. But God has revealed enough for us to trust him and obey him: 'The secret things belong to the LORD our God, but the things revealed belong to us and to our children for ever, that we may follow all the words of this law' (Deuteronomy 29:29).

Do we really trust him, or is it only when things are going well? Do we really obey him, or only when it suits us to do so? The Bible likens this testing process to gold being refined in the fire (1 Peter 1:7): a painful process in which the dross (the rubbish in our life) is removed and the quality, the pure gold, the purity of heart, is what remains . . . forever.

The redoubtable American Christian educator Henrietta Mears, whose life had such a profound impact on Christian leaders such as Billy Graham and Bill Bright, was reportedly asked on her deathbed whether she would have done things differently. Her reply: 'If I had to do it all over again, I would have trusted Christ more.'

God can be trusted, Father, Son and Holy Spirit. I hope that at the end of my life I can say what Paul said at the end of his: 'I know whom I have believed, and am convinced that he is able to guard what I have entrusted to him until that day' (2 Timothy 1:12).

It is as we learn to trust God day by day that the gap between our profession of faith and the way we live closes.

Reflection

Christian faith is not complicated. It involves trusting God completely.

In what ways do you find it difficult to trust God right now?

If God is a loving Father, why do I not trust him? Why am I so anxious about anything?

Read and meditate on the promises of God to provide, lead and protect you. Try some of these:

Deuteronomy 31:8
Psalm 55:22
Philippians 4:6–7
Hebrews 13:5
1 Peter 5:7

Commit each area of your life to him each day.

11. Hoping for the best?

Weeping may stay for the night,
but rejoicing comes in the morning.
(Psalm 30:5)

I remain confident of this:
I will see the goodness of the LORD
in the land of the living.
(Psalm 27:13)

The gap between what is and what will be

Faith, hope and love (1 Corinthians 13:13): according to the apostle Paul, these are the three things that last, the three things that matter when the chips are down. The greatest of these is love, because it is the essence of God's character (1 John 4:7) and the basis of relationships as God intends them to be. Faith (that is, saving faith in God through Christ) is more precious than gold (1 Peter 1:7), and it is the power that overcomes all that this godless world can throw at us (1 John 5:5). Hope is to look forward, with joyful anticipation rather than fear or foreboding, to the future fulfilment of God's promises.

If faith is trust in the unseen God (Hebrews 11:1), then hope is focused on what our unseen God has in store for us

– something far better (Philippians 1:23). If faith bridges the gap between what is seen and what is unseen, then hope is the link between what is now and what will be. Without hope, there is no lasting joy in life.

In Western secular culture, there is a great emphasis on 'living for the moment' or 'living in the moment'. Certainly, God calls us to live in the moment, by being thankful each day for his goodness, seizing the opportunities before us, using the gifts he has given and relying each day on his grace. As we have seen in chapter 7, it is wise to recognize that life is short and uncertain (Psalm 90:12). But if we forget or ignore the prospect of life beyond the grave, then we are like a blinkered horse, shutting out a whole dimension of reality from our vision, and with no view of the finishing line. We naturally spend most of our time and energy grappling with the day-to-day issues of life – what is happening now. But we need to pay greater attention to what will be, to our future hope, in its full biblical meaning.

Hope

When the Bible speaks of hope, it does not mean wishful thinking, or positive thinking. It does not mean 'hoping for the best'. Rather, it has the sense of waiting and longing for the fulfilment of God's promises. Little children may say, 'I can't wait for my birthday tomorrow.' Yes, they can, because tomorrow will come – they just have to wait. We too have to wait for what God has promised.

We all know what it is to have to wait for something we are longing for – an exam result, news from an interview, or just a holiday. My late father had to wait over a year for a cataract operation. Every day he would wake up, hoping to receive a phone call or a letter summoning him to the hospital for an operation that would restore his sight. It was a long, frustrating wait, but eventually the call came.

We also know what it is to hope longingly for something we would like to have, but which, realistically, we have very little chance of receiving. We may dream of winning the Lotto; we may long for a certain job, or hope for a date with a particular member of the opposite sex!

It's nice to be optimistic and see the bright side of any situation, to see the glass half full rather than half empty. But if we base our life on unreal expectations, we will end up disillusioned.

So Christian hope is not wishful thinking, not just looking on the bright side. It is longing to see God's promises fulfilled, and waiting, as we look forward patiently, expectantly, to the day when they will be.

Hope and human experience

Hope, joy and suffering are often intertwined in Scripture and in our experience. Paul raises the issue of suffering in one of the most joyful, hopeful and uplifting chapters in the whole Bible. Romans 8 begins: 'Therefore, there is now no condemnation for those who are in Christ Jesus.' Paul goes on to talk about freedom from the law's condemnation (8:2), the life-giving power of the Holy Spirit (verse 4), the assurance of eternal life (verse 11), the security of belonging to God's family and being one of his children (verse 14), and the privilege of being able to call God 'Father' (verse 15).

Then comes a stark reminder of the state of the world and of suffering, from which Christians are not immune. If I asked you to stop reading and write down a list of the problems you are facing right now and the worries that crowd into your mind, you would not find that difficult. The former Australian prime minister, Sir Malcolm Fraser, once commented, 'Life was not meant to be easy.' That struck a chord with many. For most of us, life is far from easy.

You may be facing loneliness, unemployment, worries at work, business or financial difficulties. You may be suffering from ill health or disability. You may have family problems, involving long-running arguments, bitterness, divorce, domestic violence or custody battles. If we look at the wider world, it could drive us to despair: ruthless dictatorships, children toting machine guns, terrorism and suicide bombers, seemingly endless disputes between Israelis and Palestinians, persecution of innocent people because of their colour, beliefs or gender.

All of this and more is what the Bible calls 'our present sufferings' (Romans 8:18). Paul is not referring here just to the persecution of Christians, which he and his generation had to endure on top of everything else. He is writing about the suffering of all people.

Dark times of despair, depression or bereavement can quickly drive a wedge between the joy and peace we sing about in church and our actual experience. How is that gap to be closed? According to the Bible, it will only be fully closed when death, the last enemy, has finally been defeated. But we do have a foretaste of that in this life, whenever we see hope triumphing over despair and death.

Certainly, Paul experienced more than his fair share of suffering, but he was also full of hope. He concludes, 'I consider that our present sufferings are not worth comparing with the glory that will be revealed in us' (Romans 8:18). When Paul uses the phrase 'I consider', he is weighing up all the pros and cons, facing the reality of the state of the world and human experience, but with his eyes firmly fixed on heaven. This is the New Testament perspective on suffering and pain. Life is not to be endured stoically, but to be lived *in hope* of the coming glory of God. This hope generates joy and enables Christians to rise above their suffering or, better, to go through the dark valley and come out on the other side.

It has become unfashionable to talk much of heaven, and most of us are more interested in improving our lives here and now. But of course, the New Testament is powerfully focused on heaven. It is only when we squarely face our mortality and the afterlife that we can make sense of life in this world. The hope that God will one day right all wrongs, sweep away the world of evil and pollution, create a new heaven and a new earth and gather his people together with him is what has enabled millions of Christians to face death without fear.

Bishop Hooper, who was burned alive in the Marian persecutions in England in the sixteenth century, went to his death with these words: 'True it is that death is bitter and life is sweet, but also consider that the death to come is more bitter and the life to come is more sweet.'[1] At that point he had become a man in whom the gap between faith and life had closed. There was no trace of hypocrisy left.

Hope for the creation

In his letter to the Romans, Paul writes about the hope and suffering, not just of the individual, but of the whole creation. He reminds us that, at the fall, 'the creation was subjected to frustration' (8:20). He means the frustration of creation not being what it was intended to be, the same frustration that led the writer of Ecclesiastes to cry out,

'Meaningless! Meaningless!' . . .
'Utterly meaningless!
    Everything is meaningless.' . . .

> All streams flow into the sea,
>> yet the sea is never full.
> (Ecclesiastes 1:1, 7)

The creation is also in 'bondage to decay' (Romans 8:21). This is not just the continuous cycle of birth, growth, aging, death and decomposition; the world itself is running down and will end. It is 'groaning', like a woman in childbirth, enduring suffering before the joy of new life (8:22).

Jesus too describes famines, wars and earthquakes on the earth as 'the beginning of birth-pains' (Matthew 24:7–8), signs that the end is coming, an end which will usher in a glorious new start. Paul goes on, 'Not only so, but we ourselves, who have the firstfruits of the Spirit, groan inwardly as we wait eagerly for our adoption to sonship, the redemption of our bodies. For in this hope we were saved' (Romans 8:23–24).

So, as Paul looks at the suffering in the world, the distress in the creation, and the future glory that God has promised to all who love him, he faces the question: How should we then live?

Living in hope

His answer is that we are to *live in hope*. This is not escapism or wishful thinking, but rather it is confident, eager anticipation of the time when all our questions will be answered, when our physical bodies (not just our spirits) will be redeemed and we will become all we were meant to be. Moreover, 'the creation itself will be liberated from its bondage to decay and brought into the freedom and glory of the children of God' (Romans 8:21).

There are two things to notice here. First, the reference to freedom. Every time we see religious activity twisted into an enslaving control mechanism, rather than a life-giving experience bringing freedom, we are to shun it. It is not from God! Second, see how big the vision of the New Testament is. This is not just about 'personal salvation'; it is about the redemption of a lost and dying world.

To live in hope is to live now, in the light of a certain future; to face the future with confidence, rather than fear. The good things to come are certain, because God has promised them. So we look forward to the promised return of Jesus: 'the blessed hope – the appearing of the glory of our great God and Saviour, Jesus Christ' (Titus 2:13).We *hope* to share in the glory of Christ, in his victory over evil. We *hope* for 'freedom and glory' (Romans 8:21), for a life which is not restricted by physical, mental or emotional weakness, or even by death. We *hope* for our adoption, when we will fully enjoy the benefits of being God's children (8:23). According to the New Testament, when you first come to faith in Christ, the Holy Spirit enters your life and assures you that you are now God's child; you have been adopted into his family. While you may know that inner conviction, it is not yet clear to all. But the day is coming, and 'the creation waits in eager expectation for the children of God to be revealed' (Romans 8:19).

All those who have been persecuted, imprisoned or laughed at, those who are worthless in the world's eyes, will one day be shown to be the privileged children of God. In Jesus' famous parable, the wheat and the weeds grow together in the field for a while, but at the harvest they will be separated (Matthew 13:24–30).

The New Testament uses three verb tenses to speak of salvation. We *have been saved* through the death of Christ; we *are being saved* as God keeps us by his grace and empowers us by his Spirit; and one day *we will be completely saved*, made whole. Our bodies, which in this life are subject to pain, disease, injury and, finally, death and decomposition, will be redeemed. This hope is *certain* because it is based on what God has promised.

In this life we have only the firstfruits of the harvest to come. We see 'the presence of the future'. But one day we will experience the real thing. In this life we have a pledge from God, just as an engagement ring signifies a promise of marriage, literally a 'betrothal gift', which, in New Testament times, once given, sealed the marriage that was going to take place. The gift of the Holy Spirit too is an irrevocable pledge, an assurance of our future (see, for example, Ephesians 1:14).

The difference hope makes

What does it mean then to live in hope? It means focusing on the future, but in the context of the present and the past; living in readiness for the end, which could come any day, with this hope permeating every part of our lives.

What difference does that make to the way we live? It does *not* mean that we are to hide our heads in the sand or tuck ourselves away in a corner, waiting for better times. Over the centuries many have taken this hopeless view of the future. If the world is fast approaching a cataclysmic finale, they say, then why worry about trying to address poverty, war or famine? If a new heaven and earth are to be created, why worry about the pollution and environmental degradation of this earth? If I am going to be like Christ in the final transformation, what does it matter how I live now?

The Bible faces these questions head-on. At the end of his second letter, Peter describes how the world will end: 'The day of the Lord will come like a thief. The heavens will disappear with a roar; the elements will be destroyed by fire, and the earth and everything done in it will be laid bare.' He goes on to ask, 'Since everything will be destroyed in this way, what kind of people ought you to be?' (2 Peter 3:10–11). Perhaps the obvious answer might be that we may as well totally give up on this life and this world.

No! The logic of the Bible takes us to quite the opposite conclusion:

> You ought to live holy and godly lives as you look forward
> to the day of God and speed its coming. That day will bring
> about the destruction of the heavens by fire, and the elements
> will melt in the heat. But in keeping with his promise we are
> looking forward to a new heaven and a new earth, where
> righteousness dwells.
> (2 Peter 3:11–13)

Some of the greatest social reforms, at least in Western society, have been brought about by Christians who had this hope within them. Think of the abolition of slavery, the Christian foundation of schools, universities and hospitals, prison reform and labour law reform – just for a start.

It was said of Samuel Rutherford, the seventeenth-century Scottish church minister, that 'he had his feet on the ground, his hand to the plough and his heart in heaven'. What a great epitaph for any Christian.

Living like this means that, as we wait and hope for God's promises to be fulfilled in the future, we also expect his promises to be fulfilled *now*, as we serve him through our work and in the daily round. It means I can live in hope that God will work in my life and in those around me, that he will answer prayer, that the church will be renewed, that relationships can be restored, that we will see some justice in this world: that gaps can be closed *now*.

In his book *The Puritan Hope*, Iain Murray illustrates the difference this hope makes to our life, using the journal of John Wesley. As an evangelist in the eighteenth century, Wesley spent much of his time with the working classes who lived in unspeakable conditions in the overcrowded city slums. He travelled to Newcastle and saw the drunkenness, violence and family breakdown that characterized the city. Even the little children had already been corrupted. But he did not throw up his hands and conclude that the situation was hopeless. He observed, 'Surely this place is ripe for Him with whom we have to do.'[2]

Wesley saw beyond the awful social conditions; he saw the opportunity and the great need for people to experience God's grace, and how this would in turn lead to a more just and compassionate society. Jesus had a similar view, when he called his disciples to open their eyes and see that the fields were ready for harvest (John 4:35).

A friend of mine was called to serve in an inner-city church in Liverpool. The area was dominated by gangs, unemployment, violence and drugs. After he had been there a while, I asked him if he was optimistic about his situation. He replied, 'I am not optimistic, but I do have hope.'

He was not just playing with words. He went on to explain that, humanly speaking, in terms of the political and social programmes in place, he was not at all optimistic that things could improve. But he had hope in God, with whom nothing is impossible; the hope that he would see the 'goodness of the LORD in the land of the living' energized him to work and serve in that hard place.

So to live in hope is much more than 'the power of positive thinking': it means looking forward to the fulfilment of God's promises, and living and acting now with that perspective. Such hope brings joy into life – even into drudgery, duty and difficulty.

Death

This Christian hope is focused strongly on life after death. The greatest challenge to the integrity of our faith and life is death – the last enemy. The Swiss theologian Kurt Marti, using Marxist terminology, described death as 'counter-revolutionary'. It is the ultimate leveller, the separator, a devastating intrusion into 'normal' life.

Death is the ultimate gap-maker. Have you ever seen or touched the dead body of someone you know and love? Until comparatively recently this was a normal experience in nearly all societies, when the infant mortality rate was high and the elderly were 'laid out' in the home prior to burial. This is still a common experience for children growing up in many countries of the world, but in most Western societies death is hidden away from us.

Death is regarded as a matter for professionals: paramedics, doctors, funeral service directors and grief counsellors. I was in my early twenties before I was confronted with death close-up. I was lazing on a beach in Mauritius, when I heard a loud shout. A boat belonging to a local fisherman, who could not swim, had capsized. He was rescued by a passing windsurfer, but he had been in the water quite some time before he was brought ashore. I tried with two others to resuscitate him for nearly half an hour, but we could not get any sign of life back.

One moment I was relaxing on the beach, the next I was holding a dead man in my arms. Death intrudes on our comfort like a very unwelcome guest.

When you touch someone's cold, dead body, you are faced with life's big questions. Where has the *life* gone? Where has the *person* gone? That's not him or her; it's just their shell. Can you really explain all this away in physiological terms? Simply by noting that the heart has stopped beating, the brain has ceased to function and therefore life has gone?

Where has the life gone? Has it simply disappeared? One moment there's a spirited, laughing, crying person; the next a cold shell, soon to decay, made from the dust of the earth and soon to return there. What happens at death? Are we extinct? Is there reincarnation of our person in another body? Or are we just a divine spark returning to the great fire, as Leo Tolstoy believed?

Resurrection

The Christian hope is not just the saving of the soul; it is the resurrection of the body. It is what Paul writes about and celebrates in the famous fifteenth chapter of his first letter to the Corinthians. He emphasizes how crucially important the bodily resurrection of Jesus Christ is to the future hope of the Christian.

When I was a student, the most common political graffiti seen around the university was the slogan: 'Che Guevara lives'. The supporters of the South American revolutionary knew he was dead, but believed that Che's ideals would live on in the next generation. They were saying that he had not lived or died in vain, that his enemies had not won.

Some think that, when the Bible speaks of resurrection, this is all it means. It was very fashionable in theological circles throughout the twentieth century to water down the gospel by arguing that what mattered was not whether Jesus *actually* rose from the dead, but rather whether or not the church *believed* he had risen. A distinction was drawn between the faith of the church on the one hand and the historical event on the other.

Paul cuts a swathe through this woolly thinking. He writes,

> If Christ has not been raised, our preaching is useless and so is your faith. More than that, we are then found to be false witnesses about God, for we have testified about God that he raised Christ from the dead. But he did not raise him if in fact the dead are not raised. For if the dead are not raised, then Christ has not been raised either. And if Christ has not been raised, your faith is futile; you are still in your sins. Then those also who have fallen asleep in Christ are lost.
>
> (1 Corinthians 15:14–18)

This is as clear as can be! If Christ did not rise from the dead, as the Bible claims, then Christians are worshipping a dead hero: there is no good news, no salvation, no assurance and, even worse, no hope. Christians are living an illusion. We may as well close all the churches and give up. Paul does not pussyfoot around here. This is too important. The Christian claim is not that Jesus lives on in our memories, or in the beliefs of the church, but that he rose, as the New Testament claims. His body was not there when the disciples went to the tomb on Easter morning. Meeting Jesus in his risen body transformed his frightened disciples into powerful public figures, who went on to suffer and die for what they knew to be true. They did not die for an academic theological construct!

Paul goes on, 'But Christ has indeed been raised from the dead, the firstfruits of those who have fallen asleep' (verse 20). Death was not the end for him. And it is not the end for us.

Christ's resurrection was like the firstfruits of the harvest; resurrection for all believers will surely follow. The harvest will be gathered. This is our future hope.

In this great passage about resurrection, Paul addresses, directly and indirectly, a number of common questions. How are the dead raised? What does a resurrection body look like? How can people rise when their bodies have rotted away or been blown apart? He answers these questions, using analogies from nature and from history. First, with an illustration from nature (verses 35–39), he explains that, when we bury a seed in the ground, the tree that grows does not look the same as the seed; but the same life is in both the acorn and the oak tree. Jesus was still recognizable in his resurrection body. In his commentary on 1 Corinthians, William Barclay wrote, 'Our earthly bodies will be buried and will dissolve – they will rise again. The form in which they rise may be different but it is the *same person* who rises.'[3]

Then Paul looks back in history to the first human, Adam. He contrasts the body of Adam, and of every human being since, with the resurrection body of the believer. Our earthly bodies are perishable, imperfect and limited.

The resurrection body (the spiritual body) is imperishable, glorious and powerful (verses 44–48), like that of the risen Christ. The gap between him and us will be closed forever.

This hope goes beyond death, giving us joy, even in the tears of a Christian funeral. This hope inspires us to keep going through all the pain of daily life, as 'we eagerly await a Saviour from [heaven] who . . . will transform our lowly bodies so that they will be like his glorious body' (Philippians 3:20–21).

This is fundamental to our faith. Jesus challenged Martha: 'I am the resurrection and the life. The one who believes in me will live, even though they die . . . Do you believe this?' (John 11:25–26). The Christian's hope is not the immortality of the soul, not just that we will live on in the memory of our family and friends, but that our bodies, created by God, will be redeemed, transformed and resurrected by his recreative power to become like Christ. Our bodies will be different, yet recognizable, unrestricted by any disability, disease, imperfection or weakness. This is the Christian hope. As Paul concludes this passage in 1 Corinthians, you can feel his excitement mounting as he writes,

> Listen, I tell you a mystery: we will not all sleep [die], but we will all be changed – in a flash, in the twinkling of an eye, at the last trumpet. For the trumpet will sound, the dead will be raised imperishable, and we will be changed. For the perishable must clothe itself with the imperishable, and the mortal with immortality . . . then the saying that is written will come true: 'Death has been swallowed up in victory.'
>
> Where, O death, is your victory?
>   Where, O death, is your sting?
> (1 Corinthians 15:51–55)

He goes on to say that the sting of death is sin. It is sin that causes death, but in the resurrection we will finally be free from the very presence of sin.

We will be able to say, in the words written on the grave of Dr Martin Luther King Jr, in Washington:

> Free at last. Free at last.
> Thank God Almighty,
> I'm free at last.

Not the end . . . not in vain

In our human experience death seems to play the last card. It creates an awful gap between us and the ones we love, a gap that seemingly cannot be bridged. Death ends beautiful lives and beautiful relationships, and leaves us lost, lonely, perplexed, shattered, empty and defeated. But *death is not the end.* Jesus rose from death and defeated this last enemy. And we will share that victory and be reunited with all who love him. In the words of C. S. Lewis:

> He [Christ] forced open a door that had been locked since the death of the first man. He has met, fought and beaten the king of death. Everything is different because He has done so. This is the beginning of the new creation – a new chapter in cosmic history has opened.[4]

After focusing on this wonderful future, Paul turns back to the reality and pressures of the world in which he is living. But as he does so, he finds in the future the inspiration needed to live a life with purpose here and now. He closes this passage with these words: 'Therefore, my dear brothers and sisters, stand firm . . . Always give yourself fully to the work of the Lord, because you know that your labour in the Lord is not in vain' (1 Corinthians 15:58).

What a contrast to the writer of Ecclesiastes, for whom most of what we do on this earth seemed pointless and without ultimate purpose! When our hope is firmly fixed on Christ, then all that we do in his name, including all the routine stuff that occupies our waking hours, is *not in vain.* That is why in another of his letters Paul gives us the key to a fulfilled life: 'Whatever you do, whether in word or deed, do it all in the name of the Lord Jesus, giving thanks to God the Father through him' (Colossians 3:17).

Death appears to be a cruel separator, but the Christian hope is that death is simply the gateway to a quality of life we can barely begin to imagine. It closes the gap between us and

God forever. Despair and depression about the state of our lives, our relationships and the world in general can sometimes appear as a huge black cloud blotting out the sun. But the God in whom we hope and trust is the One who raises the dead. He breathes new life into people who are spiritually dead, and into dying churches. He is the God who has promised to triumph over all evil, and he pours his resurrection power into our lives on this earth to enable us to triumph over all the experiences that would separate us from him: sin, despair, depression – even death itself.

Reflection

Read Romans 8:28–39.

Are you afraid to die? If so, why?

In what ways is God calling you to put your hope wholly in him?

PART 5:
THE GAP IS CLOSED . . .
AS WE NEAR OUR GOAL

12. Eyes on the prize

I press on to take hold of that for which
Christ Jesus took hold of me.
(Philippians 3:12)

The gap between us and the finishing line

The Bible likens the Christian life both to a journey and to a
long-distance race. There is a goal to be reached and a prize
to be won. The problems are all around, and the destination
is far off. We don't know when the end will come. We can't
see the God who guides us along the way, and we frequently
lose our direction. The people we have to journey with can
be difficult. Sometimes our commitment wavers and we are
unsure whether it is all worthwhile.

The temptation is always there to give up, to stop worrying
about the gaps, to stop grappling with the big problems that
impinge on our lives, to sink back into dull mediocrity and to
become resigned to the way things are.

But thank God, he has a better way for us!

We are to keep our eyes on the prize and *hold on*, to keep
our eyes on the prize and *press on*. The prize is being welcomed
into the presence of God at the end. It is to know and understand God in all his glory and to be changed, to become like
him; to enjoy for all eternity a perfect relationship with others
and with God himself; to enjoy the new creation that God will

make. The prize is to be with Christ who loved us and died for us, and to enjoy that forever.

Imagine: no more gaps between you and God; no more gaps between you and others; no misunderstandings, tensions, resentments, jealousies, envy, fear, revenge, cruelty; no more gaps within you as a person. Instead, consistency and wholeness; no more fear, doubt or anxiety; no more feeling that you are being pulled in two directions at once; no more worry about living up to other people's expectations or facing impossible demands. Just imagine being fully at peace with yourself, full of thankfulness.

Think how you have felt in your very best moments: that's a foretaste of heaven. Think of times when you felt very close to another person; or when you have felt overwhelmed by the beauty of God's creation and in harmony with it all; or a time of prayer or worship when God's presence has been very real to you. Those are all foretastes of heaven.

The day is coming when we shall be like Jesus, when all wrongs will be righted, evil conquered, and the gap between God and his people will be closed forever. That's why we are encouraged to keep our eyes on the prize and to keep going.

Sadly, some Christians give up and end their lives bitter and disillusioned. In this chapter, I want us to explore why this happens, and also draw out the biblical encouragement and inspiration to keep going. As we do so, let's dip into the letter to the Hebrews, written to Christians who were in danger of giving up.

Why do people give up?

When a long-standing relationship breaks up, a friendship, a marriage, or a business partnership, outsiders are often left wondering how it happened. Was there a slow, gradual drifting apart, or was there some point at which the ways parted and the different objectives and values of each party became obvious? Was there a single act of betrayal? Or a gradual build-up of smaller issues? It's often so hard to understand, because relationships, like life, are so complicated.

This is also the case when there is a breakdown in someone's relationship with God. When we see a previously strong professing Christian who is no longer interested in the Bible or in fellowship, and who is no longer trusting in God, we are left wondering how this could have happened. As with human relationships, it's often hard to disentangle cause and effect.

Do people lose their faith because they stop praying and reading their Bible? Or do they stop praying and reading the Bible because they have lost their faith? Do people stop coming to worship because their relationship with God has grown cold? Or do they grow cold because they have stopped coming to worship? Do we become more selfish, unloving and difficult to live with because we have lost our sense of joy in the Holy Spirit? Or do we lose our joy because we have become more difficult as people?

One thing is certain. When we start to lose our faith, our love of Scripture and our desire to pray and worship, the important thing is not that we can precisely pinpoint the cause, but that we take action to fix the problem.

The term 'affirmative action' was coined by the women's liberation movement in the twentieth century for a proactive programme to win equal rights for women in the workplace. Affirmative action of a different type is needed when we start to slip down the slope away from God.

The letter to the Hebrews was written to people who were losing their faith and on the verge of giving up. They were so confused, worn down and overwhelmed by life that they were struggling to keep going. Maybe you are in that position or at least know someone who is.

Hebrews is full of warnings about the dangers of giving up. God warns us, because he cares. If you see a child playing near the edge of a crumbling clifftop, aren't you going to warn them to move away? So if our heavenly Father sees us slipping into dangerous situations, he will send us a strong warning: 'Watch out!' In Hebrews, though, we have much more than warnings; we also have encouragement to keep going and to *do something* about the gaps we have allowed to open up between us and God. We are also continually pointed towards the Lord Jesus Christ, the Son at God's right hand. He is the perfect sacrifice for our sin, the High Priest who can sympathize with our weakness, the pioneer and perfecter of our faith, who is the same yesterday, today and forever.

Warnings

The first warning is about *drifting*: 'We must pay the most careful attention, therefore, to what we have heard [the Word of God], so that we do not drift away' (2:1). Drifting is slow and often imperceptible. A boat may gradually start to drift from its mooring as its knot becomes loose.

In one of my early attempts at windsurfing, I recall gliding over the water away from the beach at high speed, feeling rather pleased with myself, only to get stranded some distance out to sea. I was then carried along helplessly by the current, and as I looked at reference points along the shore, it was a shock to see how far I had drifted.

Think about your relationship with God with reference to your past. Do you find yourself gradually attending church less frequently? Have you stopped reading your Bible? Have you lost your motivation to perform acts of service for others?

Check how far you may have drifted: look at some reference points – where were you one year ago, or five years ago, or ten? Drifting is a passive experience. We are carried along by forces outside ourselves. It's not that we are paddling in the wrong direction, but that we are doing nothing. The effects of our inaction are serious.

Using a different illustration, Jesus told the story of two builders, one who built on rock and one on sand. When the storms came, only the house built on rock survived. Jesus' punchline is penetrating: 'Everyone who hears these words of mine and does not put them into practice is like a foolish man who built his house on sand' (Matthew 7:26). Notice carefully what he is saying. What do we have to do to keep building on the sand? Answer – nothing; just ignore Jesus' teaching. But to do nothing is, paradoxically, to put another brick down on the sand for a building that will not weather the storm that is coming.

The warning here is one that a schoolteacher might give: 'Pay attention!' We must pay attention to what we have heard, to the gospel, to the grace of God revealed in Jesus Christ and in the Scriptures. Perhaps you need God's wake-up call to stop drifting through life and get back on the path he has set for you.

The second picture in Hebrews is one of a *break-up in a relationship*. 'See to it . . . that none of you has a sinful, unbelieving heart that *turns away* from the living God' (3:12, italics mine). This is not a slow, gradual drift, nor is it passive inaction. This is a decisive, deliberate turning away: the spiritual equivalent of adultery. It happens when what God provides no longer satisfies my needs or when what God has done for me does not seem to be of any value. I no longer want to follow where he is leading, so I turn away.

Where do I turn? Typically, to my career, my business, my own home-made religion, or to a belief system that makes fewer demands. Sometimes I meet people who have turned away from the Christian faith. 'I used to believe like you,' they say, 'but now I have moved on.' This turning away may feed our pride and ego in the short term, but it deceives us and hardens us. Hebrews recalls the story of the wilderness wanderings of the people of Israel when they turned against God in the desert, and warns us to learn from their mistakes:

> Today, if you hear his voice,
>> do not harden your hearts.
>
> (3:7–8)

God is always wanting to speak to us through his Word and by his Spirit, always calling us back when we have strayed. We need to listen, to get back to studying Scripture and applying it day by day.

The third picture is one of *falling short*, of giving up before reaching the appointed end of the journey. Again the writer calls to mind the way in which the great majority of the people who set out from Egypt never entered the Promised Land. They gave up trusting God and were not allowed to enter. Only Caleb and Joshua made it, because they continued to trust God. They were both wholehearted, undivided in their commitment.

The danger in any long race is that we will give up before the finish. When the struggle gets hard, cramp sets in, breathing becomes difficult and our body aches. The temptation to stop running is enormous. At that point, we may lose sight of the goal for which we have trained for years and forget the rewards that will follow. This is not drifting or turning away. This is just not being prepared to put in the effort any longer. Sometimes in the Christian life we will be tempted to give up; the journey will seem too arduous, the race too long, the effort required too great – so that I simply stop.

If that describes your experience right now, then thank God that he can get you moving again. Stopping is not irreversible! We do not race against one another. Our goal is to complete the course. Picture the marathon runner who 'hits the wall', stops for a drink, walks a few paces, and then, remembering how far she has come, how much she wants to finish and spurred on by the shouts of support from the sideline, starts running again with renewed determination.

The fourth picture is of *losing our hold*. Sometimes we may feel that our faith is failing, that we are dangling over a cliff, holding on to a rope. Our strength and will to keep holding on are failing and we are tempted to end the struggle and let go. We may feel that it is us holding on to God, rather than the other way round, and that we no longer have the mental or spiritual energy to do that. It is much less effort just to give up. What would you shout to a person dangling over a cliff face holding on to a rope for dear life? 'Hold on! Hold on! Help is coming!'

So it is with God. His encouragement to us is just to hold on and never give up (see Hebrews 3:6, 14). Similarly, we are called to encourage others who are in danger of losing their hold and to remember that God is holding on to us (Psalm 73:23).

'Has your faith ever been tested?' That question was thrown at me in a discussion group at a friend's home. 'Yes . . . it has . . . many times'. It turned out that the young woman asking the question had recently lost her baby and had nearly lost her faith. She felt she was hanging on to God by a thread and rapidly losing her hold. As a group, we spent the rest of the evening listening to the woman's story, sharing about our own testing times and encouraging one another in the light of God's great love.

The final picture in Hebrews on this theme of giving up is that of *throwing away*. 'Do not throw away your confidence [in Christ]; it will be richly rewarded. You need to persevere . . . ' (10:35–36). We throw things away when they are no longer of any value or of any use: old clothes and ornaments, broken computers or TV sets. Sometimes people throw away things that they think are of no value but which turn out to be priceless. Some have discarded their faith as no longer of any value to them. But to discard the one thing in all the world that is of most value is a huge mistake. Your faith is 'of greater worth than gold' (1 Peter 1:7). There is nothing more precious than an eternal relationship with God. Don't throw it away.

These five vivid pictures, of drifting, turning away, falling short, losing hold and throwing away, are all warnings from a loving God not to give up, however hard it may seem to us at the moment. They are also intended to encourage us to keep going.

Encouragements

Sometimes one word of encouragement is worth more than many warnings. Wise parents and teachers know that. So does our heavenly Father.

This letter to the Hebrews is meant to encourage us. It also calls us to 'encourage one another daily' (3:13). Many of us spend our days full of anxiety, wondering how we are going to cope. God knows that we always need encouragement. Many of the words of encouragement in Hebrews are exhortations to *do* something. Note that these don't take the form of instructions and directions, as in, 'You must . . . ', but rather they urge concerted, inclusive action, such as: 'Let us . . . ' Here are some of them.

'Let us, therefore, make every effort to enter that rest' (4:11)
The goal is supremely worthwhile: enjoying the love of God and the presence of God is what we were created for. It is worth any amount of effort on our part. Don't give up just because the going gets tough. Whatever your age, if you are a Christian, the best is not behind you; it is still to come.

'Let us hold firmly to the faith we profess' (4:14)
Why? Because we have a great High Priest, Jesus the Son of God, who understands our weaknesses and was tempted just like we are (4:15). He too was tempted to give up and to run a different course from the one set for him (Matthew 4:1–11; 16:22–23; 26:36–42).

I once belonged to a small church which seemed to have more than its fair share of problems. Almost every family and individual member was hurting in one way or another due to bereavement, divorce, children with drug problems, redundancy, financial difficulties, and other issues weighing them down. In one worship service, the leader asked us (rhetorically) what our goals were for the year. 'As for me,' he said, 'I just want to survive.' Sometimes that is how we feel, and we need to encourage one another in those situations, not with superficial Christian platitudes, but with the deep truths of the Word of God and with practical demonstrations of the love of God.

What encouraging words have you spoken today?

'Let us then approach God's throne of grace with confidence, so that we may receive mercy and find grace to help us in our time of need' (4:16)
Let's remind ourselves, and one another, of the great privilege of knowing God and of being welcomed into his presence. Notice the order: mercy first and then grace. We usually come

to God with a long list of things we want him to do for us. But it seems that at the top of God's list is bringing us back to acknowledge our sin, our need of a Saviour and *to receive his mercy.*

I often get that the wrong way round and lose my sense of proportion. My problems loom very large, and God may seem small and distant. But as I have had to return to God many times after wandering off, I have found that a restored relationship with him and enjoying his forgiveness become much more important than my pressing issues. As I come to 'the throne of grace', I get my problems back into perspective.

'Let us move beyond the elementary teachings about Christ and be taken forward to maturity' (6:1)

It's not that we are to forget or treat lightly the wonderful simple truths of the Christian gospel, which change lives, but we do need to realize that there is always more to learn. God means us to grow in the grace and knowledge of him (2 Peter 3:18). What are you doing to grow in your knowledge of God? What are you doing to help others grow?

'Let us draw near to God with a sincere heart and with the full assurance that faith brings' (10:22)

Here is a call to respond daily to the gracious invitation of our Father, who bids us to come to him with empty hands through his Son and bring to him our prayers and our lives. Let's keep praying, confident that we have access to the God who rules the whole universe.

'Let us hold unswervingly to the hope we profess, for he who promised is faithful' (10:23)

God will not let us down. He will fulfil all his promises in his good time.

The late Dr Martyn Lloyd-Jones, after retiring from his ministry at Westminster Chapel in London, used to preach regularly at churches around the UK and further afield. After one such service at a new, struggling church, 'the Doctor' was greeting people. To everyone he met, he gave the same words of encouragement: 'Keep going; press on; God is faithful.'

My friend was surprised that this was all the great man had to say. He had expected some great insights or words of wisdom. But later, as my friend reflected on the evening, it was these words that stayed with him. He came to the conclusion that this was the best encouragement of all. Keep going. 'He who promised is faithful.'

'Let us consider how we may spur one another on towards love and good deeds' (10:24)

Notice our role here is to encourage one another, to get the best out of one another, and not put one another down.

When I first became a Christian in Africa, there was a lot in my life that was quite obviously not consistent with a Christian lifestyle. I shall always be grateful for those wise leaders and new Christian friends who, rather than pointing out all my shortcomings, kept encouraging me to get to know the Lord better. God had other ways of making me aware of my faults. He had given me his Spirit to change me.

Sometimes God's encouragement to us comes not in words but in an experience of his Holy Spirit, reassuring us of his love and power. And sometimes encouragement comes just through the presence of others.

About halfway through our six years in Mauritius, several of our closest friends left the island around the same time. As young Christians, we had leaned on these people and had learned so much from them. Their departure left a huge gap in our lives, and we were feeling bereft and very low.

After a few months, a young married couple from Canada arrived, and we immediately developed a strong bond with them. We prayed together, relaxed together and worked together, helping the churches on the island in various ways. I remember reading the words of the apostle Paul: 'But God, who comforts the downcast, comforted us by the coming of Titus' (2 Corinthians 7:6). I knew exactly what he meant. God certainly encouraged and strengthened us by the arrival in Mauritius of these two special people.

'Let us . . . not [give] up meeting together' (10:24–25)

We need to belong to a group of Christians, to a church where we can share in worship and prayer, where we can both give and receive practical support. Some people criticize Christians for being weak, for needing a religious crutch and not having the guts to face life alone. The truth is that our Creator never meant us to manage by ourselves. We need God and we need one another; like different parts of a body (1 Corinthians 12), like members of a family.

My wife and I have worshipped in many different churches around the world. In almost every place, we have joined a small home group, where we have found lasting friendships and support. It is in such groups that 'fellowship' becomes a reality, as we learn from and encourage one another.

There was one notable exception, however. For a period of several years, we allowed our busy work and family schedule to squeeze out time for any midweek meeting. Looking back, those years were the most lifeless, dry period of our lives, and we were much poorer for it.

'Encouraging one another – and all the more as you see the Day approaching' (10:25)

Notice the encouragement here is to keep going because the

end is in sight, the Day of the Lord's return. It is an undeniable truism for the Christian that 'our salvation is nearer now than when we first believed' (Romans 13:11).

Most of us avoid thinking about death, and I suspect not many of us really live each day looking forward to the Lord's return. In one Christian meeting, we were asked whether we could really pray the prayer: 'Come, Lord Jesus' with sincerity. One man replied, 'I want the Lord to come, but not until after our overseas holiday. We have been planning and looking forward to it for such a long time!' Was he being flippant or just honest? Let's not get too pious or overcritical here. But perhaps we do need to encourage one another to think more about how wonderful Christ's return will be for the believer:

> 'What no eye has seen,
>   what no ear has heard,
> and what no human mind has conceived' –
>   the things God has prepared for those who love him.
> (1 Corinthians 2:9)

Any form of encouragement usually brightens our day. This morning I shared a coffee with a retired minister in Australia. I told him about the uncertainties of our present situation: Where should we live? What did God have in store for us? He said with a warm smile, 'I think the God who is running the universe has that project under control, don't you?' It was not a put-down. It was a timely reminder of God's faithfulness and a great encouragement to me.

'Let us throw off everything that hinders and the sin that so easily entangles' (12:1)

I find it all too easy to fill my days with things that are not important, to accumulate more possessions than I need, and to let life become unnecessarily complicated. My natural sin-fulness of course contributes to that complexity, particularly in relationships. Here is a call and an encouragement to make life simpler, to review priorities, to have a regular clean-up of my life, to confess sin, to restore relationships and to run free!

'Let us run with perseverance the race marked out for us' (12:1)

God has set a course for each of us to run. My course is different from yours, but the finishing line is the same, and we each have the same companion and leader. No-one else can run your race for you, but you do not run by yourself. Christ has promised to be with us all the way.

One of the ways we can encourage people is by sharing what God has done for us and in us. I have always found it uplifting to hear people from very different cultures, age groups and backgrounds share how they came to faith in Christ and how Christ has led them through 'many dangers, toils and snares'. It always encourages me to keep going on the course God has marked out for me.

'Fixing our eyes on Jesus, the pioneer and perfecter of faith' (12:2)

The greatest thing we can do for another human being is to point them to Jesus, the Alpha and Omega, the beginning and the end. He is the only Saviour, Mediator, Lord and King. I have listened to many sermons and talks over the years. Some have taught me a lot; some have promised me new experiences. Some have inspired me; others have bored me or even angered me. But the ones I remember with gratitude are those that have shown me more of Jesus Christ; those that have not just given me 'Bible information', theological concepts or 'blessed thoughts', but have made Christ real to me by faithfully expounding and applying the Bible.

Sometimes, in the face of the onslaught of aggressive atheism and materialism permeating Western societies, in the plurality of religious messages in our multicultural world, or as we look at the many public failings of the institutional church, we can easily become confused in our thinking about God. We can start to drift, to loosen our hold, to give up or even turn away from our faith. If you are at that point now, then the most important thing in the whole world is to get your focus back on the Lord Jesus Christ.

Throughout Hebrews, God warns, encourages and inspires us. Our inspiration comes from looking to Jesus. Three times in the letter, our eyes and our minds are drawn to him: 'Fix your thoughts on Jesus . . . ' (3:1); 'Fixing our eyes on Jesus . . . ' (12:2); and 'Consider him . . . ' (12:3). He is the unique Son of God (1:1–2), obedient to the will of his Father (5:5), and faithful in all God gave him to do. He is the Saviour (7:25), the Good Shepherd (13:20) and 'the same yesterday and today and for ever' (13:8).

If we stick close to Jesus, we will not go far wrong.

Reflection

What do you value most highly in life?

In what ways and in what situations have you been tempted to give up the Christian faith, your Christian witness and service?

Reread the letter to the Hebrews. What encouragement do you find there to keep going?

Who can you encourage today?

13. Conclusion: Closing the gap

Because my servant Caleb has a different
spirit and follows me wholeheartedly,
I will bring him into the land . . .
(Numbers 14:24)

Gaps closed or closing?

This book began with a seemingly negative experience, a low point in my Christian life. But it drove me back to seek God through reading the Scriptures. The gaps in my life, relationships and expectations were clearly exposed, and I had to face up to them and find answers.

Like me, you may be very conscious of the gaps: between the world as it is and as we would like it to be; between the church as it is and as it could be; the gaps in our relationships that we seem unable or unwilling to close; the gaps between the people we want to be and the people we are; and, of course, the gap between us and God.

These gaps are obvious. But as we lift our heads up above the mess, we realize that God is at work closing these gaps. He has brought us to know him. He is changing us into his likeness. He enables us to build relationships that reflect his character and make a difference for good in this world. He guides and keeps us through testing times.

But what is our role in all this? How do we fit in with God's plans?

Two things I have learned from the Bible as I grapple with these questions: First, God intends us to enjoy the peace of mind and sense of purpose that come from understanding what he has done, what he will do and what he is doing now in the world: a three-way perspective.

Second, he calls us to a 'whole-heart' commitment to him, to live an 'undivided life'.

A three-way perspective

I love walking high up in the mountains. Recently I realized a long-standing ambition to trek in the Himalayas. It was hard work. Our guide jokingly referred to our trail as 'Nepali flat', because of the endless ups and downs. The mountain scenery was stunning, but there were daily challenges: the high altitude, the unrelenting slog, the diet and general feelings of nausea that came and went.

My wife and I both needed encouragement to keep going at different times. Sometimes, just to pause and *look back down* to the valley from which we had climbed was very encouraging. 'Look how far we have come! What a fantastic view!' Sometimes we paused to *look up* to the magnificent mountain peaks, to remind ourselves of where we were heading. With every upward step, we moved closer to our goal. At other times *the experience of the moment* was encouragement in itself: meeting people, enjoying the incredible mountain scenery, the wild flowers and bird life, and sharing experiences with our guide about family, work and beliefs.

I found the whole unforgettable experience of that trek to be a great parable. God encourages us when we look *back* at the past (at what he has done), *around* at the present (at what he is doing in our life now) and *forward* to the future (at what he has promised he will do).

For example, Paul writes, 'Therefore, since we have been justified through faith [past], we have peace with God through our Lord Jesus Christ [present] . . . And we boast in the hope of the glory of God [future]' (Romans 5:1–2).

This is surely how God means us to live: on the firm foundation of what he has done, with hope and expectation at what he will do, and enjoying now the daily experience of his guidance, strength and presence.

Looking back

The message of the Christian gospel is first and foremost about *what God has done*. This message runs right through the Bible, but it is summed up beautifully by the apostle Paul: 'But God demonstrates his own love for us in this: while we were still sinners, Christ died for us' (Romans 5:8).

Look at how much is contained in these two short phrases. 'Christ died': that's a fact of history. His death was 'for us': God has revealed to us its purpose and meaning. It was 'while we were still sinners', telling us that God loves us as we are and has acted in love before we ever gave him a thought. Furthermore, Christ's death, and God's act of love in sending his own Son, 'demonstrates his own love for us'.

When my wife first came to faith in Christ after we had met in Tanzania, it was the realization that there was nothing *she* could do to get right with God that marked the turning point. She recognized with great relief and thankfulness that she had only to respond to what God had already done for her. She learned that salvation is a free gift that cannot be earned.

It is an indication of human pride and sinfulness that we have such difficulty accepting this, and such difficulty in remembering it. I find it amazing how quickly I default back to trying to earn 'Brownie points' with God. I need frequent reminders that the foundation for my life is on what God has done for me in Christ, not on what I do or will do.

We are also encouraged to look back to *how God has led us in the past*; to remember how he has brought us through many testing times, answered many prayers and surprised us with his grace (see, for example, Deuteronomy 8:18; Ephesians 2:12).

How do we do that? Maybe we could start a journal to record how God has answered prayers, or perhaps phone or email a friend to encourage them.

Recently my wife and I received an email from someone whose name we did not recognize. He had acquired our email address from 'a friend of a friend' and wrote to say how God had spoken to him in a life-changing moment at a Bible study in our home *some thirty years ago*! We racked our brains but could not remember the evening that was so memorable to him. We had no idea at all of what had happened that had had such an impact on this man's life, but we found it wonderfully encouraging, both that God had worked in his life in such a lasting way, and that he had thought to encourage us by sharing his experience.

God is always doing more in people's lives than we are aware of.

The present

What about now? Just this week we received news from a friend, whose husband had died a few months ago, to say that her daughter had lost her baby, seven months into her pregnancy. Another friend emailed asking for prayer about a difficult situation with his neighbour which was making daily life a nightmare. Another friend phoned in tears to say that her husband's health was deteriorating. All are Christian believers. All are 'doing it tough'. What is the good news?

God has not left us alone – he will see us through. Wonderfully, all three went on to share about the strength they are finding in God.

When our world seems to be collapsing around us, the God who loved us enough to give his Son will not abandon us. Paul reminds us, 'If God is for us, who can be against us? He who did not spare his own Son, but gave him up for us all – how will he not also, along with him, graciously give us all things?' (Romans 8:31–32). Because God has done the *greater* thing in giving his Son, we can be sure that he will do the *lesser* thing, keeping us through the trials of this life.

God is at work, bringing people to know him. European humanists keep proudly predicting the end of Christianity, claiming that the old religious myths will soon fade away, but the church seems to be growing rapidly almost everywhere, except in Europe!

My work has taken me to several different countries. I have had the privilege of seeing people from various cultures come to faith in Jesus Christ. At a recent service in the Middle East, I heard testimonies from a Chilean, a Nigerian and a Pakistani, all of whom had come to faith in Christ in different places and in a variety of ways. God continues to build his church of true believers in every culture.

God often surprises us. One Sunday morning, a Scottish woman, whom we had known for years, announced quietly that she had given her life to Christ. It was like a bolt from the blue. She was quiet and self-contained, and not the sort of person who liked to talk about religion. But God had worked in her life by his Spirit, and she was changed in a lasting way.

Looking forward

We also need to keep looking *forward* to the goal, to the day when the race will be over and the victory finally won. As we saw in the last chapter, we need to keep our eyes on the prize and look forward expectantly to the time when all gaps will be closed.

The apostle Paul expressed it like this: 'But one thing I do: forgetting what is behind [i.e. past failure and even past success] and straining towards what is ahead [when all gaps will be closed], I press on towards the goal to win the prize for which God has called me heavenwards in Christ Jesus' (Philippians 3:13–14).

Paul did not mean that he was forgetting all that Christ had done for him in the past. He gave thanks for that continually, as all his letters make clear. But he always kept in sight the future glory that God had promised, and that was a tremendous motivation for him when he faced opposition. He lived with that great balance that comes from a focus on the past and the future and then, in the present, finding in God the power, direction and energy to live purposefully each day.

When I lose sight of what God has done for me and focus only on the present, it is like moving off the solid rock onto the shifting sand. I start to take the gospel for granted. When I stop looking forward, I lose the joy and sense of purpose of knowing where I am heading. If I no longer rely on God's grace in the present and try to live self-sufficiently, I start to miss out on seeing God at work.

This three-way perspective is fundamental to our faith and to our worship. When we share in Holy Communion, the Bible directs us to look in these three directions as we come to worship God. As we take the bread and wine, we look back in remembrance of Jesus' death for us. We look forwards, as Jesus himself did at the last supper, to the ultimate coming of

God's kingdom when we will drink the new wine together with him. We are also encouraged to look around us, in the present, to realize that we are part of the body of Christ, members one with another, and we are to live in interdependence on one another and relying on God's grace.

A whole-heart commitment

Sometimes life can be a mess, with bits and pieces all over the place.

How can we bring it all together and live with integrity? When we try to unpick the muddle, we often find that we are pulled in too many directions, trying to do too many things and trying to please too many people. We discover that there are dark 'no-go' areas of our lives from which we try to exclude God and that we certainly don't want other people to see. We find we have lost our joy in being God's person. Our commitment to him is at best half-hearted.

Let me end this book with one of the most inspiring views of the Christian life in all of Scripture. In Paul's letter to the Colossians, he keeps using words like 'all', 'every', 'complete', 'united', 'whole', and inclusive words like 'whatever' to show us an undivided life and how it is to be lived. To highlight this, these words appear in italics in the passages below.

An undivided life acknowledges the total supremacy and sovereignty of the Lord Jesus Christ. The Bible reveals to us this breathtaking picture of who Jesus Christ really is:

> The Son is the image of the invisible God, the firstborn over *all* creation. For in him *all* things were created . . . *all* things have been created through him and for him. He is before *all* things, and in him *all* things hold together . . . For God was pleased to have *all* his fullness dwell in him, and through him to reconcile

to himself *all* things, whether things on earth or things in
heaven, by making peace through his blood, shed on the cross.
(1:15–20)

An undivided life begins and grows through a faith relationship with Jesus. Paul explains the purpose of his ministry in
preaching the Christian gospel.

My goal is that they may be encouraged in heart and united in love,
so that they may have the *full* riches of *complete* understanding, in
order that they may know the mystery of God, namely Christ,
in whom are hidden *all* the treasures of wisdom and knowledge.
(2:2–3)

Paul goes on to explain what Christ has done for us: 'God
made you alive with Christ. He forgave us *all* our sins' (2:13).
Moreover, 'In Christ you have been brought to fullness. He is
the head over *every* power and authority' (2:10).

An undivided life involves a ruthless dealing with sin in
our life:

Put to death, therefore, *whatever* belongs to your earthly nature
. . . now you must also rid yourself of *all* such things as these:
anger, rage, malice, slander, and filthy language from your lips.
(3:5, 8)

An undivided life transforms relationships:

Bear with each other and forgive one another if any of you has
a grievance against someone. Forgive as the Lord forgave you.
And over all these virtues put on love, which binds them *all*
together in *perfect unity*.
(3:13–14)

It affects all we say and do: 'Whatever you do, whether in word or deed, do it *all* in the name of the Lord Jesus, giving thanks to God the Father through him' (3:17).

It affects the way we work: 'Whatever you do, work at it with *all* your heart, as working for the Lord, not for human masters' (3:23).

It affects the way we conduct ourselves in this godless world: 'Be wise in the way you act towards outsiders; make the most of every opportunity. Let your conversation be always full of grace . . . ' (4:5–6).

Jesus summed up the undivided life in two memorable sentences: 'Love the Lord your God with *all* your heart and with *all* your soul and with *all* your mind . . . Love your neighbour as yourself' (Matthew 22:37, 39).

He uses the word 'all' three times. Nothing is excluded. He wants total commitment. This is a message that God wants us to hear and understand. An undivided life involves total commitment: every area of our life is Christ's.

So how are we to respond? Do we carry on with a half-hearted faith, withholding whole areas of our life from God, and continuing in our broken relationships and a stop-start commitment? Or do we want to change? Do we want to be made whole?

Can we make that choice? Can we pray, with the psalmist?

Teach me your way, LORD,
    that I may rely on your faithfulness;
give me an undivided heart,
    that I may fear your name.
(Psalm 86:11, italics mine)

Notes

Preface

1. Bob Dylan, 'Blind Willie McTell'. Copyright ©1983, Special Rider Music.

1. The problem

1. Taken from a short story by Adrian Plass, 'Nothing But the Truth', *Father to the Man and Other Stories* (HarperCollins, 1997).
2. Stephen Rand, *Guinea Pig for Lunch* (Hodder & Stoughton, 1998), page number unknown, italics mine.
3. Stuart Townend and Keith Getty, 'In Christ Alone'. Copyright © 2001, Thankyou Music.

2. Facing the truth

1. See J. Luft and H. Ingham, *The Johari Window: A Graphic Model of Interpersonal Awareness* (UCLA, 1955).

3. Loving change

1. This is a common paraphrase of a comment by John Newton, as quoted in *The Christian Spectator*, vol. 3 (1821), p. 186.
2. R. D. Laing, *The Divided Self: An Existential Study in Sanity and Madness* (Penguin, 1960).
3. Pamela Stephenson, *Billy* (HarperCollins, 2001), p. 3, italics mine.
4. 'Calon Lân': http://www.wikipedia.org/wiki/Calon_Lân.

5. *The Homilies of S. John Chrysostom on the Second Epistle of St. Paul the Apostle to the Corinthians* (John Henry Parker, 1848), p. 111.
6. The source is unknown, but it is variously attributed to John Bunyan, by Corrie Ten Boon, and to John Berridge (1716–93), by Charles H. Spurgeon.
7. Source unknown.

4. Growing relationships

1. Cynthia Lennon, *John* (Hodder & Stoughton, 2005), from the Foreword by Julian Lennon, p. xi.
2. C. S. Lewis, *Mere Christianity* (Collins, 2012), p. 16.
3. The *Mail on Sunday*, 15 February 2009.
4. *Daily Mail*, 16 November 2010: http://www.dailymail.co.uk/news/article-1330033/Yacht-husband-Paul-Chandler-told-Your-father-died-kidnapped.html (accessed 18 December 2012).
5. Paul Sangster, *Doctor Sangster* (Epworth Press, 1962), p. 345.

5. Working it out

1. C. H. Spurgeon, Sermons on Proverbs, 'One Lion, Two Lions, No Lion at All!', sermon no. 1670, delivered on Thursday evening, 8 June 1882, at the Metropolitan Tabernacle, Newington: http://www.ccel.org/ccel/spurgeon/proverbs.txt (accessed 7 January 2013).
2. Joel Bakan, *The Corporation* (Constable, 2005), p. 54.
3. Mark Greene, *The Great Divide* (LICC, 2010).
4. http://www.kellyservices.com.au/AU/About-Us/News-Room/March-10-11-top-five-reasons-employees-leave-their-jobs/?terms=leave%20their%20jobs.
5. George Herbert, 'The Elixir', *The Temple* (1633).

8. Enjoying success

1. Geoffrey W. Bromiley (ed.), *International Standard Bible Encyclopedia*, 4 vols (Eerdmans, 1989), p. 1012.

9. Recovering from failure

1. Taken from a speech by J. K. Rowling, entitled 'The Fringe Benefits of Failure, and the Importance of Imagination', Harvard University, 5 June 2008: http://harvardmagazine.com/2008/06/the-fringe-benefits-failure-the-importance-imagination (accessed 18 February 2013).

10. Tested faith

1. Sheila Hancock, *The Two of Us: My Life with John Thaw* (Bloomsbury, 2004), p. 127.
2. D. A. Carson, *How Long, O Lord? Reflections on Suffering and Evil* (IVP, 2006), p. 159.
3. Günter Rutenborn, *The Sign of Jonah* (The Lutheran Student Association of America, 1954), pp. 29–31.
4. For readers wishing to explore this issue in more depth, D. A. Carson's book *How Long, O Lord?* is a helpful start.
5. Carson, *How Long*, p. 159.
6. Elisabeth Elliot, *God's Guidance: A Slow and Certain Light* (Revell, 1997).
7. John Newton, 'The Lord Will Provide', *Olney Hymns* (1779).

11. Hoping for the best?

1. 'The History, Imprisonment, and Examination of Mr. John Hooper, Bishop of Worcester and Gloucester', *Foxe's Book of Martyrs* (1563).
2. Iain Murray, *The Puritan Hope* (Banner of Truth, 1975), page number unknown.
3. William Barclay, *The Letter to the Corinthians* (Westminster John Knox, 2002), p. 185.
4. C. S. Lewis, *Miracles: A Preliminary Study* (Macmillan, 1965), p. 150.

For more information about IVP
and our publications visit
www.ivpbooks.com

Get regular updates at **ivpbooks.com/signup**
Find us on **facebook.com/ivpbooks**
Follow us on **twitter.com/ivpbookcentre**

Inter-Varsity Press, a company limited by guarantee registered in England and Wales, number 05202650. Registered office IVP Bookcentre, Norton Street, Nottingham NG7 3HR, United Kingdom. Registered charity number 1105757.